North Side State Bank is pleased to present to the

citizens of our fine community this beautiful

pictorial history of Sweetwater County.

Proceeds from this limited edition volume will go to benefit

the Sweetwater County Museum Foundation.

Wide open spaces and unusual geology contribute to Sweetwater County's uniqueness.

Historical Images of
SWEETWATER COUNTY

by
A. Dudley Gardner
&
Val Brinkerhoff
edited by Jolane Culhane

THE
DONNING COMPANY
PUBLISHERS

Unless otherwise noted, all historic photographs are reproduced courtesy of the Sweetwater County Historical Museum, Green River. On all photographs, if quotations are used, the phrases within the quotes appear on the back of the original photograph provided by the Sweetwater County Historical Museum. The exceptions to ownership rights are the 1950 Union Pacific Coal Mine photographs which come from Western Wyoming College's collection. Other exceptions to ownership are indicated in the captions of the individual photograph.

Illustrations by Sharon Love

Dedicated to Dr. William R. Snell and Dr. Richard W. Etulain, wise scholars and gentlemen who have given me more than I can ever repay.

The Donning Company/Publishers
184 Business Park Drive, Suite 106
Virginia Beach, VA 23462

At the Donning Company/Publishers:
Steve Mull, General Manager
Elizabeth B. Bobbitt, Editor
Mary Eliza Midgett, Designer
Barbara A. Bolton, Project Director
Tracey Emmons-Schneider, Project Research Coordinator

Library of Congress Cataloging in Publication Data:
Gardner, A. Dudley.
    Historical Images of Sweetwater County / by A. Dudley Gardner and Val
Brinkerhoff ; edited by Jolane Culhane.
        p. cm.
    Includes bibliographical references and index.
    ISBN 0-89865-877-2 (alk. paper)
    1. Sweetwater County (Wyo.)—Pictorial works. 2. Sweetwater County (Wyo.)—
History. I. Brinkerhoff, Val, 1956– II. Culhane, Jolane. III. Title.
    F767. S9G38 1993   93-11716
        978.7'85—dc20   CIP
Printed in the United States of America

Contents

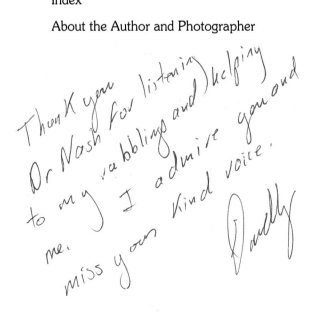

Thank you for listening
Dr Nash (and helping)
to my rabbling and helping
me. I admire you and
miss your kind voice.

Dudly

Preface and Acknowledgments

We had a toilsome day before us of twenty miles to the little Sandy one of the Waters of the Green River . . . . We decided to take the [Sublette] cutoff and drove over an arid plain to Big Sandy. . . . We found good grass on the Big Sandy, and here we again threw away superfluous articles. . . . The desert over which we were to pass was an arid plain, without a drop of water, or a blade of grass, the soil being of soft, dry, ashy consistence. The dust was an impalpable powder, and the dense clouds which arose almost produced suffocation.

A. Delano, July 1, 1854[1]

The road from Sandy to Green River is well lined with dead cattle and horses, and we passed many live ones left by their owners which must soon die as they can get no water, though they might yet find a little bunch of grass. The Wind River Mountains in the northeast and a long range of Mountains to the south are white with snow. Those to the north but a short distance off and are timbered with pine or other evergreens, but no timber on the plains. Nothing but bare hills with the most savage and desolate aspect imaginable. There is a grandeur and sublimity in a view from some of these hills that you look in vanity for elsewhere.

Bryan N. McKinstry, July 13, 1850[2]

Nineteenth-century travelers through present Sweetwater County were tired and travel weary by the time they reached the wide high mountain desert. Their trip west to Utah, Oregon, or California was not complete. They were in passage to somewhere else. For Bryan

---

The "Killpecker Dune" field was formed sometime around 20,000 to 7,500 B.P. or at the end of the last ice age. While this date is debated by some, it appears the sand dunes of Sweetwater County began to form near the end of the last glacial period. Fencing, found periodically throughout the area, is used to stop drifting into various natural gas and oil well sites. This photograph was taken roughly thirty miles northeast of Rock Springs.

The Green River Valley was the site of Rendezvous, ferries, stage stations, and ranches. John Wesley Powell's famed 1869 expedition began near this spot.

N. McKinstry and A. Delano, they were only halfway there. As much or more lay ahead as lay behind. The travelers still faced the deserts of the Great Basin. To these nineteenth-century sojourners, southwest Wyoming was something to cross and they recorded their toil from the perspective of strangers only traversing the land. Through filters of dust that the wagons stirred around them, they looked at a place unfamiliar to them. There could be little wonder that they viewed this strange land with jaded eyes. They were simply passing through and saw the land in terms of outsiders. Yet, for all their complaints, they did appreciate the "grandeur and sublimity" of the landscape broken only by the distant and towering snow-capped mountains. The sagebrush-covered basin could be breathtakingly beautiful. But in the mid-1800s, people had to be concerned with losing their lives or their livestock to an environment that might, if not understood, be unforgiving.

The perceptions of southwestern Wyoming too often have been recorded by people with no ties to the soil, those simply passing through with no intention of staying. Whether it is an interstate traveler wondering the distance to the next gas station or motel, or a nineteenth-century railroad passenger bored by long hours of traveling in a small space, a person passing through only catches a glimpse of a much wider picture; they see only parts of the land that are not understood by simply passing through.

Sweetwater County is beautiful. It is part of a desert. For some people, it is their place of birth. The idea of a birthplace being important is a significant concept in some countries, but not in mobile America. For a society accustomed to moving rapidly from place to place and rarely having its life cycle begin and end in one location, understanding how an area can become a point of reference can be a difficult concept to grasp. Here sage and barren hills can be more beautiful than dense forests. In fact, travelers away from Rock Springs often joke when they return from the East Coast or

Pacific Northwest that "they couldn't see anything, there were too many trees blocking the view." That perception is based on place. To prefer one area over another does not necessarily mean one is provincial, it means the person understands what he or she is viewing. Shifting sand, stark and barren canyon walls, sagebrush meadows filled with wildlife are all part of this place—a place that contains "grandeur and sublimity of view."

There are hundreds of ways to view Sweetwater County. This work presents a few historical images designed to capture part of the past. It has become difficult, due to the growth in the number of historical publications and the emergence of thousands of new pieces of primary sources, for any one person to report on even small segments of the past, and this is my excuse for the inadequacies in this account. In particular, this work is limited in size due to publication requirements. That is no excuse for inadequacies, but points to the limitations. To present this material in the space given, I have focused on a few historic processes and the landscape. More work is needed on the history of Wyoming, and I look forward to the day when a history of women, Slovenians, Serbs, and Scots of Sweetwater County is written. Moreover, a history of trona mining, natural gas development, and uranium mining is also needed. This work can only touch on these topics and not address them.

The people of Sweetwater County have long labored to make this county a place apart. Isolated, yet tied to the nation by trails, the first transcontinental railroad, and one of the nation's first transcontinental highways, the county is distinctive. There may well be no other county like Sweetwater County. The nature of its mines and landscape help set it apart. And only a few other counties in the state of Wyoming have the racial and ethnic diversity evident in the state's largest county. It is this distinctiveness that drew me to this place. It is for my friends and neighbors that I attempt to tell this tale of the past.

Boar's Tusk, north of Rock Springs, is a unique volcanic feature that rises as an isolated spire above the Killpecker Creek Valley floor.

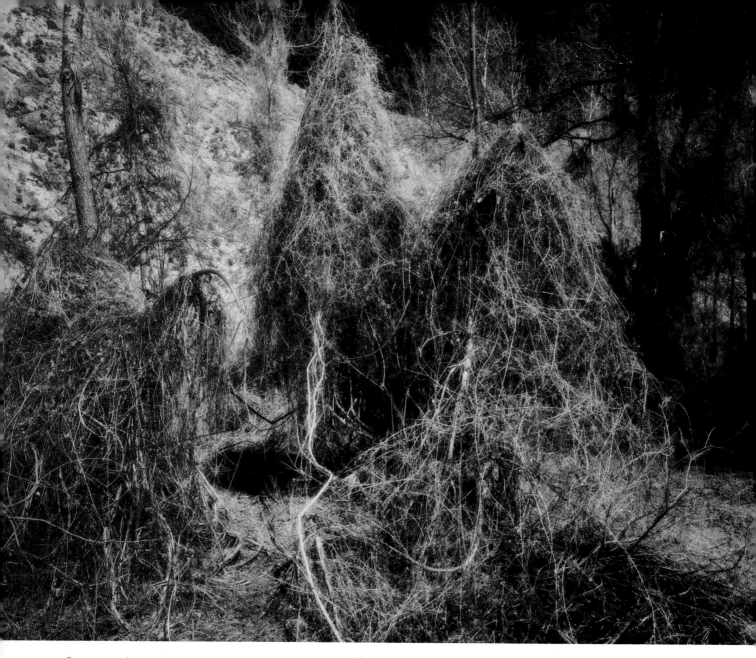

Cottonwood trees line the well-watered banks of Green River. But immediately west, as is shown here, the desert recaptures the land.

No work is ever written without incurring debts to numerous individuals. A photographic history, especially, relies on the aid of many. This work has been in the process of being written for nearly two years. In that time, many have helped. To Dr. Howard Rabinowitz, I am especially indebted for his attempts to teach an old dog like me new tricks. This endeavor requires much patience, more so than training a young mind, but this he is doing and has done. And to tolerant professors who bore with me as I burst into their offices unannounced and who listened to me, thank you for never being anything but patient. To Dr. Gerald D. Nash, Dr. Margaret Connell-Szasz, Dr. Virginia Scharff, Dr. Linda Hall, Dr. Ferenc Szasz and Dr. Noel Pugach, thank you for your warm hearts and brilliant insights into the past.

Dave Johnson, Ruth Lauritzen, Mark Nelson, Jon Hunner, and John Anselmi all read and commented on the content of this work.

Frank Prevedel, Russel Tanner, Verla Flores, Kevin Thompson, Jana Pastor, Jim Beveridge, Debbie Braithwaite, Bud and Mary Tebedo, Dave Kathka, Fred Radosevich, Christian Bunning, William Fabian, Mark Kurtz, Linda Taliaferro, Larry Caller, Kathy Karpan, Collen Altaffer-Smith, Jackie Freeze, Kathy Gilbert, Ray Lovato, Roger Varley, and Tex Boggs all influenced this work in many ways. Dr. John Collins and Chris Plant aided in researching this effort and helped lead this work to the final production as did Betsy Bobbitt at the Donning Company, Publishers. Past and present Sweetwater County historians such as Henry Chady, Ora Wright and Lenora Wright, and Linda Simnacher have made it easier to undertake this effort.

This book was written while I was on sabbatical at the University of New Mexico. The History Department was more than supportive. I will greatly miss the department, but Wyoming is my home. To Dr. Richard Berthold, Dr. James Boone, Dr. Melissa Bokovoy, Dr. Jane Slaughter, Dr. Melvin Yazawa, and Dr. Jonathan Porter, thank you for intellectual freedom and stimulating discourse that helped me see the world from a fresh perspective and with more clarity. One day I hope to repay your kindness. And to Ev, Ferrante, Abbe, Bill, Tom, Jon, Scott, Jeff, Roxanne, Yvonne, Liz, Bryan, Sandy, Yolanda, Juliet, Maggie, and Benny—bless you from the bottom of my heart. In spite of all the help I have received, some lessons I am still learning and all errors here are the sole responsibility of the author.

In Wyoming, my life makes more sense to me. It is in Sweetwater County where the West of imagination, for me, still exists. It is here that Jodie, Will, and Emma reside. It is here that my old friends and students share in the scenery of stars on a silent desert night. Friends such as Paul Ng, Betty Ng, Debbie Allen, and Mike Allen have given me much including the rare gift of their time and concern. And to the typist, Phyllis, and her husband and assistant, Gary, I wish you would both move to Rock Springs.

Dudley Gardner
April 15, 1993

A sea of sand held by a snow fence.

Introduction

First there was the land, next the Native Americans, and then the others whose relatives' roots were from distant shores, but always the land. The land and how people lived on it are what set Sweetwater County apart from all other places. This cultural landscape makes the area unique. The history of Sweetwater County begins with the Indians and their lands. In the years between 1803 and 1868, southwestern Wyoming was the homeland of the Shoshoni Nation. It was their homeland throughout their tribal history. Through the heart of that land ran the Seedskadee River. *Seedskadee,* which means sage hen or prairie chicken, was called *Rio Verde del Norte* by the Spanish and the Green River by American fur trappers. The latter name marked the maps of government surveyors and railroad builders, and identifies the river today. Like the original name of the river, the people who first lived here are too frequently forgotten. But even as the casual observer can still see the canyons cut by the ancient Green River, so too can the present-day observer see the marks the Shoshonis made on the land. Like the Flaming Gorge Canyon, cut by the waters of the Seedskadee, the river and the Shoshonis carved messages in stone. The river did so by cutting downward, the Shoshonis by pecking pictures of mountain sheep, buffalo, and horses on rock outcroppings. When one views these rock art panels drawn on stone, the question emerges: Who left these marks? This question is answered by studying pictures of the past.

East of Rock Springs and south of Bitter Creek stands a low dividing ridge that the Overland Trail crosses. Along this ridge grows beeweed, a violet flower atop a long green stem. Some stalks are covered with violet, others have only one flower. Yet the flowers stand in contrast to the brown soil, the tan late-summer grasses, and gray-green sage.

In mid or late summer, when the grass dries on the stalk, some of the last of the desert flowers emerge, not for the purpose of standing in contrast against the brown, but because it is their time.

Moving sands in the Killpecker Dune Field north of Rock Springs. The dunes provide recreation for locals and a habitat for a variety of wildlife including a unique herd of desert elk.

Long gone are the evening primrose, the flowering phlox, and the light reddish-yellow flowers of the prickly pear cactus. Now is time for beeweeds to bloom.

The Indians knew that in a few short weeks, beeweed flowers would leave pods containing small, edible peas. And so they came to this ridge, just as people do today, for that food. Beneath the beeweed, are flakes, tiny chips of stone that have fallen here, left by people who came generations before the descendants of Europeans ever reached Rock Springs.

These fallen pieces of stone convey messages. These messages, inadvertently left, lie near where the beeweed now blooms. The chipped stones, some red, others dull brown, lying on the desert floor, remind us that the descendants of Europeans or Asians from distant shores were not the first to inhibit this quiet ridge. Shoshonis, Utes, and Bannocks were here first; they called this place home.

The desert appears harsh, but is actually delicate. Oregon-bound pioneers, California argonauts, and Mormons seeking a desert kingdom passed near this beeweed-covered ridge side.[1] Their wagon wheels left scars and burned deep ruts into a land that appears harsh, yet is as fragile as violet flowers in the desert.

Sweetwater County is like this desert country, seemingly barren yet teeming with life. One need only look at the ground to see that life abounds in miniature. Short sagebrush, phlox, and tiny shoots of grass are here. In spring, meadow grass and broad-leafed plants, called forbs, emerge green and succulent in isolated parts of the desert. Pronghorn (antelope), mule deer, and elk feed on the fresh green grass found in the sagebrush desert. These green plants provide life-giving nutrients critical to the development of animal embryos. When an antelope or deer fawn is born, survival depends on the amount and quality of its mother's milk, which in turn depends on her intake of succulent green grasses. These grasses also provide the moisture needed for insect reproduction. Insects abound in the seemingly endless sagebrush expanses in the months of May and June. Almost all birds require insects for food if they are to produce healthy eggs and young. The newly hatched birds consume large numbers of insects to insure their survival and growth.

In fall and winter, sagebrush also provides the food and cover needed for wildlife to survive in the desert. The grasses have dried but still contain the nutrition needed to keep Wyoming's wildlife abundant. Here, in this desert, life for some of the largest mammals in North America begins and ends. The desert, though a broad expanse of wide open spaces, is not empty.

I have discovered, as a student of western history, that perceptions of the West vary widely. To some it is a hunter's paradise, an old theme trappers first espoused, next English sportsmen, and more recently modern hunting enthusiasts. For me, however, the West is a region of working people, men and women working in its wide open expanses atop oil rigs, underground in trona mines, or even driving trucks on the interstate. Still, what I love about the West is as idyllic as the ideals of others. I like the vast open spaces dotted by the remains of Native American villages and of ghost towns, the latter of which were once prosperous mining or farming communities.

My fondest memories and cherished times are those of early fall. During these fall days, sun-drenching but gradually cooling, I still walk out across the desert to find the remains of the past. Sometimes on the sides of hills, frequently etched in sandstone cliffs, or existing along the flanks of moving sand dunes, remnants of those who passed by earlier are yet evident. After mapping, photographing, and pondering why they came and why they left, I climb into my truck and drive down a two-track road into darkness. Intrigued with my research, I've forgotten the time and that evening will soon engulf me. Traveling homeward and looking across a moon-drenched desert landscape where no other headlights or human activities pierce the dark makes me reflective. The road too rough for me to hear my tape player, I stop the truck and listen to the voiceless silence and look at a sky filled with tiny white lights. I realize again that I live here because of the desert and the silent nights.

In Sweetwater County, the richness of this unique past makes the pursuit of history especially enjoyable, even though understanding how the historic patterns fit together is not easy. In fact, at times explaining the past is like chasing a fast-moving shadow across the desert floor only to find that once one catches up to it, the shadow vanishes. Similarly, Sweetwater County is a complex place of moving shadows reflecting a past that cannot be totally explained.

This work presents but a snapshot of a complex, wonderful place; it will provide only a brief discussion of a rich heritage, only one view of a historical past that is wonderful and exciting. The photographs illustrate major themes, not all aspects of this rich past. Indeed the photographs are like the rock art left by the Shoshonis: they pose as many questions as they answer. Still, these photographs provide a visual clue to the past's rich textures. In the end, like the rock flakes scattered on the floor near the violet flowers of late summer, they are an indication of past activity in Sweetwater County, intended as part of the picture, but not the whole story.

Chapter I
NATIVE AMERICANS,
FUR TRAPPERS,
AND EMIGRANTS

All of what would become southwest Wyoming was affected by similar patterns. To describe the early history of Sweetwater County before the arrival of the transcontinental railroad, one must look at a wider area. Interactions between Native Americans and fur trappers and traders mark the beginning of the area's written history. By the 1840s, traders and trappers began to make southwestern Wyoming their permanent home. It was in the 1840s that westward-bound emigrants began to pass through the area by the hundreds; by the end of the decade, thousands of emigrants were passing through future Sweetwater County bound either for Utah, California, or the Oregon Territory.

The Indians who lived in southwestern Wyoming when the fur trappers arrived belonged to three tribes. Their boundary lines were marked by mountains and rivers, but their borders were not drawn on maps. The Western Wyoming Range divided Bannock from Shoshoni lands; yet, Bannocks commonly traveled to the Green River to hunt and trade with the first trappers, and later with westward-bound emigrants. The Uinta Mountains served as the boundary between the Shoshonis and Utes; but Utes commonly crossed the mountains to trade at Fort Bridger. Southwestern Wyoming was an international borderland with Shoshonis, Bannocks, and Utes claiming portions of the future state. It was the Shoshonis, however, who lived in future Sweetwater County with Utes claiming the southern fringes along the Colorado and Utah border.

For the Shoshonis, the acquisition of the horse was one of the most important events in their tribal history. With the horse they could range farther both to hunt and trade and potentially enrich themselves with needed trade goods and more food. Sometime around 1700, the Shoshonis gained the horse. This altered their

Wagons on the desert continue to provide a sense of Sweetwater County's past.

way of life forever. Now they were able to travel farther out into the plains in search of buffalo. They were also able to hunt buffalo in southwestern Wyoming more easily. In the Green River Basin, stretching from Pinedale to south of the town of Green River, vast herds of buffalo roamed. The herds, although not as large as those found on the plains, were sizeable. In July of 1832, Warren Angus Ferris descended into the northern end of the Green River Valley and said the "plain was literally covered with buffalo."[1] Eighteen years later, Howard Stansbury reported seeing buffalo near the Haystacks south of present Wamsutter. At this point, Stansbury writes: "Several buffalo were seen to-day, and one antelope killed. Our hunters are calculating upon the sport before us as we approach buffalo range . . . ."[2] (Within quotations the original punctuation, spelling, and capitalization is used.)

The first residents of Sweetwater County were Native Americans. The sun symbol shown here is a common motif in the carvings of the area.

This petroglyph or rock drawing (meaning pecked into stone) reflects a horse-mounted warrior wearing a headdress and carrying a spear. Clearly seen here is a man on his horse, a common figure drawn by Native Americans in the region.

So important was the horse to the Shoshonis' way of life that they began to modify their culture to accommodate an economy based on hunting from the back of a horse. This change was reflected in the art and objects they manufactured. Carved on the stone of Sweetwater County are pictures of horses, animals the Indians dearly loved and needed. Rock art throughout southwest Wyoming shows how important the horse was. Native Americans would peck, chisel, or paint warriors mounted on horses on the sandstone of Sweetwater County. The rock art shows not only horses, but warriors riding these animals. Some of the illustrations look similar to ones drawn on stone on the Great Plains. The rocks provide proof that other Native American groups traveled into southwestern Wyoming. The written records kept by white men confirm that Sioux, Crows, Arapahos, and Cheyennes traveled through the area on horses. Not only Plains Indians, but Blackfeet from the Northern Rockies and Navajos from the Southwest were known to visit the area in the years between 1825 and 1868.

For the Shoshonis, hunting and trading was an important part of their economy. These great traders first exchanged goods with fur trappers, then with westward-bound emigrants. Through shrewd trading, the Shoshonis acquired large herds of horses. Trappers and

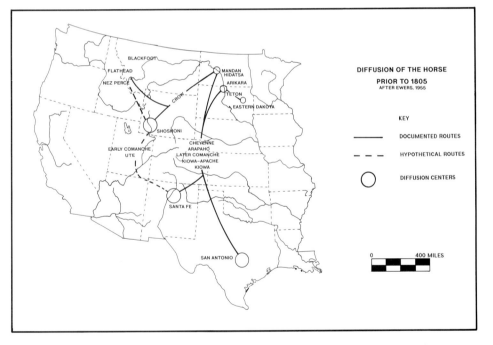

The horse played a major role in the life of Native Americans in southwestern Wyoming. Routes on map show how the horse spread from the Southwest to present southern Wyoming. John C. Ewers speculates that southwest Wyoming was a major diffusion center from which the horse spread throughout the intermountain West.

Native American artists pecked complex motifs into stone. In this grouping buffalo, men, and other unclear figures fill the large panel. The date of creation is uncertain, but the presence of figures on horses in a nearby panel suggest a date after 1700, which archaeologists suggest as consistent with the arrival of the horse in southwestern Wyoming.

emigrants often commented on the size of their herds, noting that the Shoshonis were among the best mounted Indians in the region. Respecting good traders, mountain men often admired the Shoshonis' talent as traders.

The basins and mountains of southwestern Wyoming were an international borderland in the years between 1824 and 1848. American, Mexican, Spanish, French, and English fur trappers and traders all worked in an area divided between six nations. In 1824 the Bannocks, Utes, Shoshonis, Mexico, Britain, and the United States all claimed parts of southwestern Wyoming. Ultimately the Bannocks, Utes, and Shoshonis, however, would have little say in how the area was divided, and the sites of future Rock Springs and Green River became part of Mexico. In fact, not until 1848 did all of Sweetwater County become part of the United States. In the years between 1803, when the Louisiana Purchase was made, and the

1848 signing of the Treaty of Guadalupe Hildago, Sweetwater County marked the northern limits of first Spain, and then Mexico. The formal boundary was the forty-second parallel and the Continental Divide. Locally, it is called tri-territories. West of the Continental Divide and south of the forty-second parallel, the land first belonged to Spain, and then Mexico. North of the forty-second parallel and west of the Continental Divide, the land was held jointly by Britain and the United States. Everything east of the Continental Divide belonged to the United States. It was in this international borderland that trappers held the first Rendezvous in 1825. These trading fairs, where trappers gained trade goods and businessmen gained furs, were open air bazaars.

On the banks of the Henry's Fork, in present Sweetwater County, the first Rendezvous was held by fur trappers in the Rocky Mountains. William Ashley located this summer Rendezvous along the lush valley of the Henry's Fork between Burnt Fork and Birch Creek.[3] James Beckworth, who attended this trading fair, wrote: "the whisky went off as free as water, even at the exorbitant price [Ashley] sold it for. All kinds of sports were indulged in with a heartiness that would astonish more civilized societies."[4] Indians, trappers, and traders traveled to what would become a yearly event to trade beaver furs for whiskey and other needed supplies. According to many accounts, the Rendezvous was a spectacle well worth witnessing. The color and romance of these mountain trade fairs was captured on canvas and by writers who wrote of these meetings of men from different nations.

This 1825 Rendezvous would not be the only Rendezvous in future Sweetwater County. In 1834, the "Ham's Fork Rendezvous"

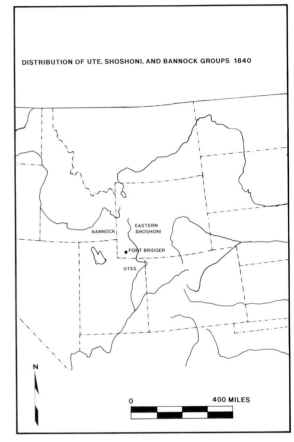

DISTRIBUTION OF UTE, SHOSHONI, AND BANNOCK GROUPS 1840

BANNOCK

EASTERN
SHOSHONI

● FORT BRIDGER

UTES

N

0   400 MILES

This map indicates the location of the three major tribal groups in southwestern Wyoming.

The complexity of a rock art panel makes interpretation problematic. At least five men and three horses are shown here. Some of the figures look very similar to those seen on the plains. Yet in some ways, this panel in Sweetwater County is unlike any found on the Great Plains or in the Great Basin. Its unique characteristics may, however, be due to the artist's own inventiveness.

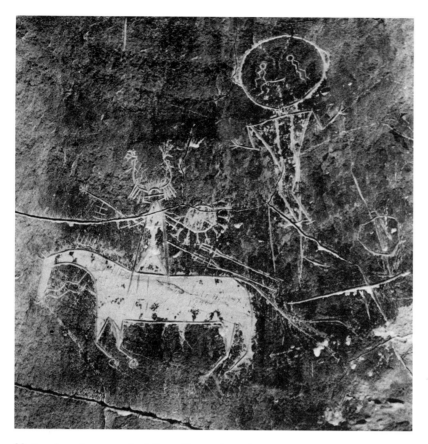

Native Americans pecked these figures into the sandstone along Bitter Creek. The weeping eye motif and the horse-mounted figure were first noted by the U.S. Army in the 1860s. One soldier carved his detachment's name and the date he visited the site near these Native American works of art. The soldier dated his visit 1868. Today, only partially visible, the year 1940 carved by another visitor appears on the horse's rear flank.

was held at four locations along the Ham's Fork River; one of these locations was near present Granger. Strung along the Ham's Fork in 1834, numerous camps were found spreading north from the confluence of the Black's Fork and Ham's Fork rivers. The Rendezvous camps moved several times to insure fresh pasture for the horses. Thomas Fitzpatrick and William Sublette made their first camp roughly five miles north of the confluence with Black and Ham's Fork.[5] An observer of the 1834 Rendezvous wrote: "The mountain men are all assembled on this river this season for Rendezvous and as crazy a set of men as I ever saw, drinking is the order of the day and trade is then best effected as, it seems, two or three glasses of grog is the best introduction to trade for, that is the time men feel the richest and can buy all the world in thirty minutes, in particular if you will trust them."[6] A variety of Native Americans and diverse nationalities were in attendance. Kirk Townsend reported, our camp "is crowded with a heterogenous assemblage of visitors. The principal of these are Indians, of the Nez Perce, Bannock and Shoshoni tribes, who come with the furs and peltries they have been collecting at the risk of their lives during the last winter and spring, to trade for ammunition, trinkets, and 'fire water'." In addition to the Native Americans, he stated, there were "French-Canadians."[7] Townsend adds, "Buffalo, antelopes, and elk are abundant in the vicinity and we are living well. We have seen also another kind of game, a beautiful bird, the size of a half grown turkey. . . ." Townsend goes on to note that these "sage chickens" were abundant in the area.[8]

Attending Rendezvous was not the only reason trappers came to future Sweetwater County. Apparently, trappers wintered in the Bitter Creek Valley near Rock Springs. Jim Bridger told Howard Stansbury, in 1850, that "the valley generally has very little snow, and has been formerly a Rendezvous for trappers and traders on account of the Buffalo."[9] Bridger, with his considerable experience in the area, noted the Bitter Creek Valley was a good place to winter. In 1841, Jim Baker reported meeting Bridger on the Henry's

Fork near the Green River.[10] Later that same year, Jim Bridger built the first Fort Bridger on the banks of the Green River in future Sweetwater County.

Jim Bridger, in partnership with Henry Fraeb, built their first fort between the Big Sandy and Black's Fork in midsummer, 1841. Lying between where these two rivers enter the Green, this trading post, built on the banks of the Green River, was a substantial outpost.[11] Edwin Bryant and William Clayton described it as having several cabins. William Lawton passing by the former trading post in 1849 "noted that cabins and chimneys were still standing and that a great quantity of cut wood gave evidence that someone had wintered there."[12] How long Bridger occupied this fort is not known. Before the post could be completed, his friend and partner Henry Fraeb was killed by Indians. Bridger, wanting to find another location for his post, moved to the Bridger Valley, where he started his second

These works of art were made by Native Americans. The figures appear to represent a male and female. On the left of this petroglyph appears the rough pecked shape of a small animal, possibly a dog.

(Top) Native Americans in downtown Rock Springs in the early 1900s.

(Bottom) The location of the major emigrant trails in southwestern Wyoming.

outpost in 1842. He soon relocated and in 1843 built his third post on the banks of the Black's Fork. This third post would become the most famous and "was later burned by the Mormons" in 1857 and then rebuilt and modified by the U.S. Army in the fall of that year.[13]

Bridger's building of his fort or trading post on the Black's Fork and the corresponding end of the trapping era roughly parallel the beginning of westward migration. The beginning of westward migration to the Pacific Coast is usually fixed at 1843. While this is an arbitrary date, it reflects the shift away from trapping and trading towards emigration through southern Wyoming. Yet neither traders nor trappers completely disappeared in 1843; in fact, many traders profited from westward-bound emigrants.

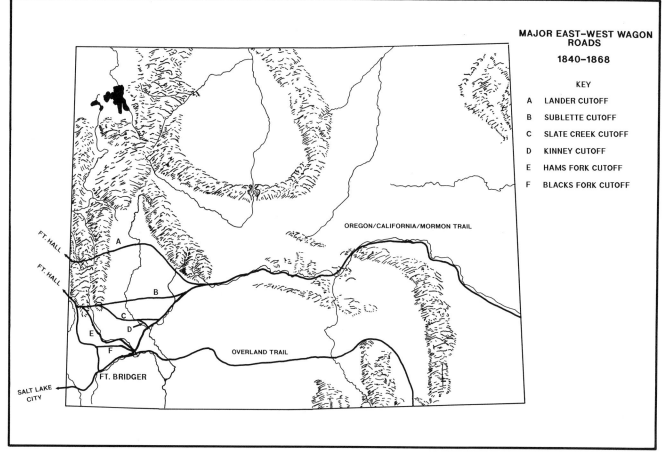

MAJOR EAST-WEST WAGON ROADS

1840-1868

KEY

A LANDER CUTOFF

B SUBLETTE CUTOFF

C SLATE CREEK CUTOFF

D KINNEY CUTOFF

E HAMS FORK CUTOFF

F BLACKS FORK CUTOFF

OREGON/CALIFORNIA/MORMON TRAIL

OVERLAND TRAIL

FT. HALL

FT. HALL

FT. BRIDGER

SALT LAKE CITY

Bridger would not be the first trader to position himself on the banks of the Green River. That distinction belongs to the women and men of the Shoshoni tribe. Stretching from LaBarge to what would be called Green River City, the Shoshonis positioned themselves to trade with westward-bound emigrants needing horses and supplies.

The Bidwell-Bartleson party was a hallmark in westward migration. In his reprint of the Bidwell diaries, historian Doyce B. Nunis states, this party "made the first planned overland emigration west to California."[14] Although other emigrants had made the overland journey to the Pacific slope via South Pass before 1841, their destination had been Oregon. "The first northern-route emigration across the plains was undertaken by Jason and Daniel Lee's small missionary band in 1834, and in 1836, by the Whitman-Spaulding party." Further south, beginning in 1829, California-bound trading caravans had ventured west by following the Santa Fe Trail and then using the Old Spanish Trail or other variants to reach the west coast. Yet no party had taken the trail traveled by "Bidwell-Bartleson and Company" in 1841.[15]

In his work, *California,* historian John W. Caughey states that the Bidwell-Bartleson party "was the entering wedge for the new type of migration to California: that is, they were bent on living permanently in the "Golden State."[16] These emigrants would cross Wyoming and follow a vague, previously untraveled route west from the Bear River to California. "Jedediah S. Smith had made the trip in 1826 and 1827, and Joseph R. Walker, employed by Captain Benjamin L. E. Bonneville, in 1833," but their reports of the way west were sketchy. There were no detailed maps or guides to tell the traveler where water could be found.[17] Setting out into the unknown, they were adventurers with a dream, but without a precise road map. As *The New Yorker* recently noted, when describing the ill-fated Donner Party that crossed Sweetwater County in 1846: "There's something about a guy with no sense of consequences that's completely American."[18] There is also something completely American about unprepared dreamers setting forth onto unknown

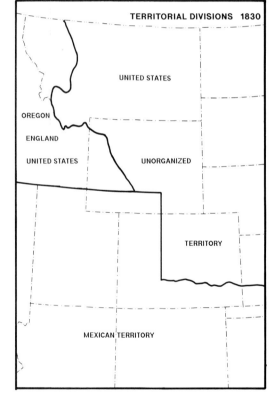

(Top) This figure carved by Native Americans may represent a turtle. Native Americans commonly carved animal figures. They expressed ideas, cultural traits, or their own personalties. They left a lasting legacy in stone.

(Bottom) Prior to 1824, the Mexican Territory was claimed by Spain. From 1824 to 1848, most of Sweetwater County would be part of Mexico.

25

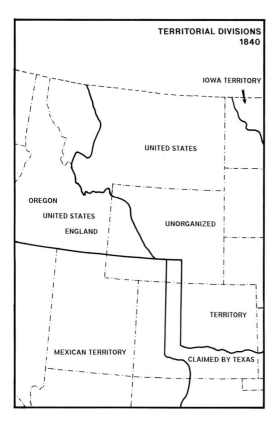

TERRITORIAL DIVISIONS
1840

IOWA TERRITORY

UNITED STATES

OREGON
UNITED STATES
ENGLAND

UNORGANIZED

TERRITORY

MEXICAN TERRITORY

CLAIMED BY TEXAS

When Texas declared her independence, portions of southwest Wyoming became part of the Republic of Texas. This map shows Wyoming in 1840.

waters and American "Indians" having to rescue them by providing them with much needed food and assistance.[19]

Reverend Joseph Williams, who was with the Bidwell-Bartleson party when it crossed the Green River in 1841, noted that the emigrants actively sought trade with the Shoshonis in southwestern Wyoming. On July 11, not far from Little Sandy Creek west of South Pass he wrote: "Today we lay by for the arrival of the Snake [Shoshoni] Indians to come and trade for articles, and a man was sent to tell them to come."[20] Thirteen days later on the Bear River the party once again "rested and waited for the Snake Indians to come and trade with us."[21] Trade was essential since their animals had worn down and food supplies were depleted. James John, who also accompanied this 1841 emigrant train, states that on the Green the travelers traded "with the Indians and Trappers for horses and buffalo robes." John adds that the trappers and Shoshonis camped with them for several days as they traveled west.[22]

In his work Plains Across, John Unruh notes that Bidwell and Bartleson "employed and even kidnapped Indians to travel with them as guides, pointing out the trail and identifying good grass and water locations." Hugh Skinner, traveling along the Hastings Cutoff in 1850, acknowledged if it hadn't been for Shoshoni Indians directing them to water they would never have found it. "Many overlanders willingly entrusted their stock, wagons, belongings and even families to Indian swimmers and boatmen at dangerous river crossings all along the trail." J. M. Shively, "explicitly stated in his 1846 guide book that 'you must hire an Indian pilot [when] you [are] at the crossings of the Snake River, it being dangerous if not perfectly understood.'"[23] While these Indian pilots and the Snake River were probably not eastern Shoshonis, the need for Indian guidance illustrates the importance Native Americans played in the westward migration.

The Shoshonis assisted Capt. John Charles Frémont in his highly publicized 1843 exploration of southwestern Wyoming and the surrounding area. When Frémont traveled along the Bear River Valley, he sought out a Shoshoni village for the purpose of trading for horses. He wrote, "we purchased eight horses, for which we gave in exchange blankets, red and blue cloth, beads, knives, and tobacco, and the usual other articles of Indian traffic." He did not reveal how many knives or blankets he gave in the exchange, but judging from the experiences of others, the cost was relatively high. Frémont also obtained from the Shoshoni "a considerable quantity of berries of different kinds, among which service berries were the most abundant;

and several kinds of roots and seeds, which we could eat with pleasure, as any kind of vegetable food was gratifying to us."[24] Frémont's remarks provide excellent insight into the problems westward-bound travelers faced. While meat abounded and the emigrants often carried flour, soon they ran out of foods containing vitamins A and C. Scurvy became a real possibility. Passing through areas that contained nutritionally rich vegetables, the emigrants and travelers did not recognize the available food sources, nor did they know how to process them. For vegetables and fruits they often turned to trading. While some emigrants picked berries they found along the trail, others were deprived of these fruits by the wagon trains that had passed before them. Therefore, trading with Native Americans proved to be an excellent way to insure adequate fruits and vegetables.

Edwin Bogart provides a revealing description of his encounter with Native Americans near the Green River crossing in 1846. On July 18 he recorded: "Several Indians visited our camp in parties of three or four at a time." Showing he did not quite comprehend their actions, he stated, "An old man and two boys sat down near the door of our tent, this morning, and there remained without speaking, but watchful of every movement for three or four hours. When dinner was over, we gave them some bread and meat, and they departed without uttering a word." The Indians were not begging, they simply were following cultural norms of polite visitation and since apparently they would not speak English and Bryant could not communicate to them in their tongue, silence seemed appropriate. Bryant did appreciate the setting he was in as he wrote: "Circles of white-tented wagons may now be seen in every direction, and the smoke from the camp-fires is curling upwards, morning, noon, and evening." A large "number of oxen and horses are scattered over the entire valley grazing upon green grass. Parties of Indians, hunters, and emigrants are galloping to and fro, and the scene is one of almost holiday liveliness." He added, "It is difficult to realize that we are in a wilderness, a thousand miles from civilization. I noticed the lupin, and a bright scarlet flower, in bloom."[25]

The Shoshonis, as well as former trappers, or hunters (as they were called in the emigrant journals), profited handsomely from trading with emigrants. At times Fort Bridger was run essentially by Native Americans. Joel Palmer, traveling west in 1845, camped near the trading post on July 25. He described the post as "built of poles and daubed with mud; it is a shabby concern." Noting the number of structures he goes on to say "Here [there] are about twenty-five lodges of Indians, or rather white trappers lodges occu-

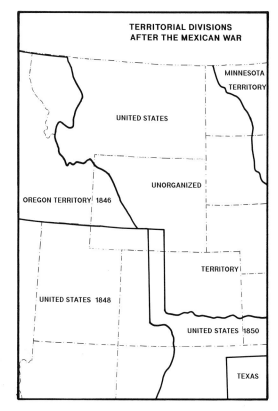

Sweetwater County was claimed by both Texas and Utah in 1848. Part of the county was in Oregon Territory.

pied by their Indian wives." They had "dressed deer, elk, and antelope skins, coats, pants, moccasins, and other Indian fixens, which they trade low for flour, pork, powder, lead, blankets, butcher-knives, spirits, hats, ready made clothes, coffee, sugar, and etc." The traders' wives were, according to Palmer, "mostly of the Pyentes and Snake Indians." For a horse, the going rate at Fort Bridger was "twenty-five to fifty dollars in trade." Since horses were often worn down by the time they reached the Bridger Valley, there was a substantial market for fresh horses."[26] Another emigrant noted that the Shoshonis sought out emigrant camps to trade their wares. In 1846, William E. Taylor wrote on July 9 "16 miles Braught us to [Fort] Bridger Shoshone in abundane [sic]." The next day the wagon train "Lay By Indians visited us in great numbers."[27]

Palmer provided yet another insight into Fort Bridger's operation and also how emigrant trade and traffic affected the area. He claimed the post was "generally abandoned . . . during the winter months."[28] Since emigrant traffic virtually ceased during the months from September to May, due to the harsh winters, it made little sense to live in the high mountain valley all winter. Following tribal traditions that had allowed the Shoshonis to thrive in this high elevation steppe, the trappers, traders, and their wives also migrated to sheltered sites better suited for enduring the longest season in the Rocky Mountains. One such site, as noted by Jim Bridger, was the confluence of Killpecker and Bitter Creeks, where present Rock Springs is located.[29] Another wintering ground was Brown's Park.

While crossing the Green River in 1849, James A. Pritchard noted an encampment of Shoshonis along the river. He wrote in his diary that the "Indians . . . had a great number of fine horses. And for which they asked a big price." He identified them as "Shoshonis or Snake Indians." "They are," according to Pritchard, "decidedly the best looking and most intelligent Indians that I ever saw. They possess an affability and suavity of manners not common to the Red Men of the Forest. Their Women are handsome delicate and genteel looking."[30] Another 1849 traveler also commented on the number of horses the Shoshoni owned. Lewis Shutterly, who traveled west in 1849, wrote "crossed Thompson's fork of green river along this is a beautiful valley and there is an Indian camp of about 200 wigwams and 1500 to 2000 Indians of the snake tribe they appear a harmless people and own many fine horses in which they take much pride they being their sole property they are remarkable good riders."[31]

At Fort Bridger on July 25, 1849, James Wilkins noted "there are here 20 or 30 families of mountaineers principally canadian French

For most of its territorial history (1850 to 1863) Sweetwater County was located in Utah Territory. Census records for 1850 and 1860 place Sweetwater County in the Green River Precinct of Utah.

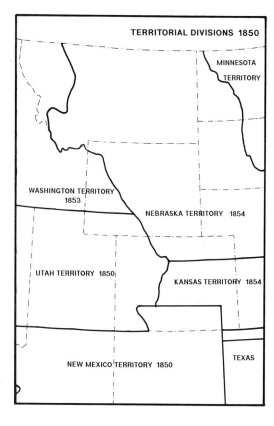

TERRITORIAL DIVISIONS 1850

MINNESOTA TERRITORY

WASHINGTON TERRITORY 1853

NEBRASKA TERRITORY 1854

UTAH TERRITORY 1850

KANSAS TERRITORY 1854

NEW MEXICO TERRITORY 1850

TEXAS

married to Indian women, and living in tents of skins. . . . " A keen observer, he added, "considerable white frost was on the ground this morn . . . Altho' there is plenty of grass and fine water, a beautiful looking trout stream close by they say they cannot raise any vegetables on account of the coldness of the nights."[32] Initially unable to grow vegetables, the residents were dependent on Native Americans for these food sources. Their use of wild plants harvested by Native Americans is also born out by the presence of Indian rice grass found in one of the storage pits within Bridger's Trading Post.[33] Indian rice grass is a desert grass found throughout southwestern Wyoming.

Writing of his trip west in 1850, Bryan McKinstry stated that at the crossing of the Ham's Fork, "Indians are plenty they are a better looking race of Indians than I have ever seen before. They are all of the Snake tribe." Noting that they had been greatly enriched by their trade with white travelers he described them: "They are whiter, better formed, better dressed, more intelligent and [own] more property than their brothers the Pawnees, Omahaws, Otoes, and etc. near the frontiers." Mounted on splendid horses the men and women "gracefully [rode] about as if they were Lords and Ladies with nothing else to do. Many are dressed in the European stile [sic], probably procured from the Emigrants or picked up." Claiming the Shoshonis were excellent traders, he explained: "they are willing to trade guns, clothes, and etc., but their horses they could not be induced to part with."[34]

Atop the Bear River Divide in western Wyoming in 1851, P. V. Crawford wrote, "Here the scenery is grand. The Green River Valley in the east and the Bear River Mountains on the west." He added, "Good grass and pure springs all the way. We met a lot of Indians today. They had been out on a hunting expedition, had plenty of game and were in good plight and good humor. Here everything is most lovely."[35] The terms used in Crawford's diary show he and his companions did not fear the Shoshonis. They were, above all, traders, and provided much needed goods and food. This is obvious in numerous diaries. As Mary Louisa Black recorded in her 1865 diary: "Aug. 2 Last night ice froze 1/8 of an inch in thickness. The Snake Indians came in to barter fish and antelope hides for bread, coffee."[36] The Shoshoni Indians consistently provided travelers with items that aided them in their trip west.

In 1843, most westward-bound emigrants crossing South Pass were headed to Oregon Territory. Passing through present Sweetwater County they traveled to Fort Bridger then turned north to Fort Hall, Idaho. Others bound west would bypass Fort Bridger and head

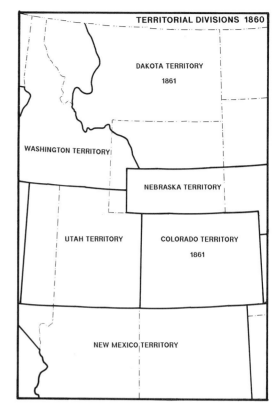

In 1860, much of Sweetwater County was part of Nebraska Territory.

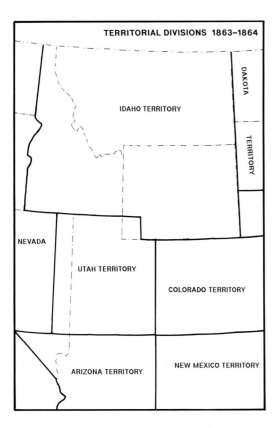

For a brief period from 1863 to 1864, Sweetwater County was part of Idaho Territory.

across the Little Colorado Desert on what would be called the Sublette Cutoff. There were other ways west in southwestern Wyoming. Travelers did not have to take the trail to Fort Bridger if they choose not to: the Ham's Fork Cutoff, Black's Fork Cutoff, and Slate Creek Cutoff all provided alternative routes west to Fort Hall. Ultimately the main trail passed through Fort Bridger, but this had more to do with where the pioneers were headed than choosing the route based on road conditions.

In 1847, Mormon pioneers followed the road to Bridger's Post on the Black's Fork and then west to the Salt Lake Valley. Most future Salt Lake bound emigrants would travel near Fort Bridger. In 1849, argonauts bound for California opted for the Sublette Cutoff, but traffic also traveled southwest to the trading post owned by Louis Vasquez and Jim Bridger. It was in 1849 that travelers tried an even more southerly route over Bridger's Pass. James Evans and Company took this route in 1849. Evans went west along Bitter Creek, and then traveled on to Fort Bridger via the Black's Fork. This route that Evans took would ultimately be known as the Overland Trail.

By the late 1850s, there were two principal ways west through future Sweetwater County. One went over South Pass and followed "the Sandy." The other traveled over Bridger's Pass then went west along Bitter Creek. Yet, no matter what road you chose you had to cross the Green River. On the banks of the Green ferrymen and their families became semi-permanent settlers. The 1860 census indicates several ferryman lived along this river. They were among the first settlers in Sweetwater County.

Overland migration was creating a long-term change in the area. The ferries on the Green River were situated along every major trail from the Lander Cutoff south to the Overland Trail near Green River City.[37] We know something about the ferries on the Green River due to census records and emigrant diaries. In 1860, the northern boundary line of the Utah Territory was situated near present LaBarge, and thus Utah census-takers concentrated their efforts on the lower ferries. On the Green River in 1860, Isaac Burbon, age twenty-three, and his wife, Clara Burbon, age eighteen, lived and owned a ferry. Clara was born in England, Isaac in Maine. The value of their property was five hundred dollars. At another unnamed ferry, William Ashboin, age twenty-five, lived by himself and his property was also valued at five hundred dollars.[38] There may have been a host of "Indian traders" strung out along the Green River in semi-permanent structures as numerous entries in the census list traders, their "wives," and children living in the precinct. Determining the traders' locations, however, is more problematic. Most traders did have "Indian wives," and the husbands' places of birth were often listed as either Canada or Washington Territory.

In addition to "Indian traders" and "ferrymen," numerous herders were reported living in the Green River Precinct in 1860.[39] While the river fixed where ferrymen had to live, traders and herders were more mobile. By 1860, southwest Wyoming was gaining the rudiments of a long-term change in who would call the region home. The military at Fort Bridger created a market for beef; emigrants traveling west created a need for services and fresh horses. Native Americans and herders gladly provided horses and supplies.

In the 1860s, change was inevitable. Initially, it came in the form of stagecoach stations, Pony Express stations, and then telegraph lines built along the Oregon Trail over South Pass. It was a fluid situation. The telegraph replaced the Pony Express and the stage stations along the South Pass route were abandoned as the stage line relocated along Bitter Creek. One constant was a stage station at South Bend (Granger). One of these stations still stands. Stagecoaches that crossed South Pass, Pony Express riders and later, Ben Holladay's stage all stopped at the Granger Stage Station. When Holladay moved the stage line south to Bitter Creek in 1862, the extant Granger Station became part of the "Overland Stage Line." From 1862 to 1868, the South Bend Station was part of the famed Overland Stage Company.

Emigrants traveling through future Sweetwater County in the 1860s could go west over the various trails. Many left records of their westward journey. The diaries describing travel over what was called the Oregon Trail describe southwestern Wyoming's landscape in ways that make the scenery of the mid-1800s recognizable today. In part, their descriptions are still vivid because the land has changed little. Unlimited vistas and wagon ruts are still evident today. Walking the trail one still sees views of the Wyoming Basin that were written about in the 1860s.

Randall H. Hewitt, who crossed South Pass by mule train in 1862, wrote that he had "crossed the great divide." He then describes a stream near his campsite. The noise of the "mad torrent, by a bank of which our camp was located, combined with that of cataracts up the stream, we cared not where made a music of an unfamiliar strain, but lulled the camp to quietness very soon after supper."[40] He noted earlier in the evening, "a rousing camp fire, a snug tent and warm blankets" on this July evening "combined to render the night not entirely comfortless. The desert beyond, par-

In 1864, most of what would become Wyoming was in Dakota Territory.

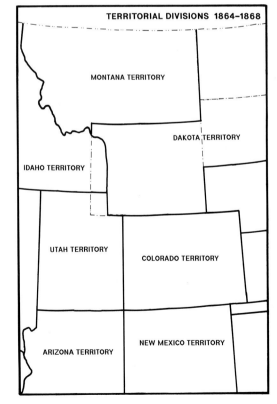

TERRITORIAL DIVISIONS 1864–1868

MONTANA TERRITORY

DAKOTA TERRITORY

IDAHO TERRITORY

UTAH TERRITORY

COLORADO TERRITORY

ARIZONA TERRITORY

NEW MEXICO TERRITORY

tially revealed from the mountains, is the Green River Valley or plains."[41] Earlier that day, Hewitt had crossed the "Little Sandy and the Big Sandy." As he went west into the "Green River Desert," he wrote, "that particular reach of . . . desert was all our fancy pictured it and very much more besides; it was desolation complete."[42]

Many nineteenth-century trail diaries possess a literary quality. Yet they are describing the area in terms of people unaccustomed to deserts and high altitudes. Many wax poetic in trying to find words to describe what they saw. One particularly vivid diary was written by a man traveling the Overland Trail in 1863. From the headwaters of Bitter Creek to a point near Church Buttes, A. Howard Cutting left a remarkable written record of a region unfamiliar to him.

This grave is found along the Overland Trail. Undated, it is typical of graves along both the Overland and Oregon Trails.

Traveling west in 1863, Cutting passed through present Rock Springs and Green River in early summer. By that time, Overland Stage stations had been built at these locations. Cutting describes many of Sweetwater County's stage stations in 1863. Cutting was a keen observer and possessed a sense of humor, something he exemplified in his description of sagebrush as "the dreariest mockery of vegetation that ever grew." He went on to claim that sagebrush "is an exotic from the Valley of Desolation, a ghost of departed brush heaps, a ghostly skeleton of a plant, of an ashy pale color, and as dry as the sand it stands in."[43]

Little is known about Cutting's origins or where he finally settled, but by June 7, 1863, he had reached the Black Butte Stage Station, south of present-day Point of Rocks. Along his entire route in early June, he was following Bitter Creek. His description of Bitter Creek was not complimentary. He does, however, give an excellent description of the valley. He writes:

June 7th. Camped at Black Butte Station about 10 o'clock. The station man here told us some bunch grass two miles off the road so we camped and took out the stock to it. Very good grass the best we have had for a long time but the water in

Bitter Creek (all we had yesterday and) all we are likely to have today is so strongly impregnated with Alkali we can hardly drink it without using Sartaric Acid or Vinegar in it. The creek the water is stagnate so low it can't run, the sides of the bank crusted . . . by the water evaporating in the sun and leaving Alkali. The water is a dirty reddish color and tastes no one can know how till they try it. We stayed here till late in the afternoon, the station men (two) treating us very kindly. Tim Connells horse sick from Alkali water also one of Boners. Gave them melted lard and vinegar. Camped at night within three miles of Rock Point. Longwell so drunk he fell of[f] his horse, and Poker had to carry him to Camp in his wagon. The water grows worse, so bad now, that even Whiskey won't help it. It gives us a kind of pain in the stomach which is hard to bear. Pokers child very sick this evening from the effects of the water.

June 8th. Poker's wife and Hetrick have a grand row and he talks rather rough to her. Passed Rock Point where there are some Sulphur Springs. The water is pretty good in comparison to Alkali water. We are passing today huge mountains of rock some of which are full of holes and crevices in which birds make their

The Overland Trail, along Bitter Creek, was first traveled by westward-bound emigrants in 1849, but in the 1860s the greatest numbers of individuals passed along the trail. These inscriptions were made in the 1860s by some of these emigrants.

Names left by westward-bound emigrants traveling west along Bitter Creek in the 1860s.

nests. These rocks remind me of lumps of furnace stone magnified. Stop at Salt Wells where we had been told we should find good grass. The Station man says two miles beyond we shall find grass. He would tell us where there was good grass if we would pay him, but we told him we know there was grass near the Station and we were going to find it. Then he said he would show us the grass, but would have to charge us for water from the well. Said they dug the well themselves and had to charge Emigrants for the water to repay them for their trouble. The grass about two miles off the road from station proves to be splendid and we decide to stay here today and let the horses have a good feast. The well water is very salt[y] and tastes and acts when used for washing just like sea water. Bureau Co. train with 49 head of stock arrive at the well bringing Tobey and his colt. The station man charges them $3.00 for watering their stock. Bitter Creek which runs directly past the well is almost unfit for any purpose, seems to grow worse the further we travel on it. A miserable lonesome country here. No wonder the stage men charge for water, should think they would need to charge for being looked at and then not get paid for staying here. This afternoon Poker and Hetrick have a grand settlement of their family troubles, and are separating their traps so they can travel each on his own individual hook in future. One of the Col's. horses gave out in the forenoon, but he has a good pair of Mules. The "Guard" for the first time, has to go two miles away from Camp to guard the stock (34) and a cold job it will be as the night's in this miserable country are extremely cold.

June 9th. Water frozen 1/2 inch thick this morning. Henry Kemper, Bob Lee, Tobey, and Pete Lauson on guard last night. They all went out to the stock taking their blankets and two only standing guard at a time, the others sleeping on the ground. Kemper and Bob stood the first part, and at 12 o'clock waked Tobey and Pete fairly up, so they went to sleep again and there was no guard after part of the night. On waking up they discovered that 20 of the animals were missing. They rode up to camp *and gave the alarm, when we soon hunted them up. Paid 15 cents a head for horses. Three times watering, 5 cents each time. Passed Rock Springs about noon, a long 14 miles from Salt Wells. Gave our stock a good drink of very bad water and flour, ate a cold lunch ourselves and pushed on for Green River 15 miles farther on, and a very long 15 miles it proved to be. [Actual distance was 17 miles according to the Overland Stage Company.] The road near here wound around among the hills so we had to travel near three miles to make one toward the river. Arrived at the river about 5 o'clock and camped on the bank. It was truly an oasis in the desert to us as we have not had water fit for a dog to drink for the last four days. Green River is a very swift stream, about 150 yards wide and too high at the present time to ford. Shall have to cross on a Ferry similar to the one on the No. Platte. This is the first respectable stream we have seen running toward the Pacific. Bitter Creek is to miserable a stream to have a name. Tho' I don't know how Emigrants would get across this desert country without it. We have some very fine view of Bluffs or rather Mountains along the river, with huge piles of rocks on their tops, looking like great towers, can see these different ones from the river crossing. The sides of the mountains are nearly as white as chalk and present a great contrast to the opposite side of the river where the hills have some signs of vegetation.*

June 10th. Crossed Green River and was on the road again by 7 1/2 o'clock. The price of crossing is $4.00 a piece for wagons and two-bits a head for horses, 1/3 off for payment in gold. Boner stays behind with his horses at this station to give him a chance to get well. Camped at noon near Black Fork or Hams Fork river. Crossed after dinner by the fork. River about a hundred yards wide and 2 1/2 feet deep. While crossing Longwells stove dropped off the back of his wagon and was rapidly floating away, when some of us behind called his attention to it otherwise he would have been minus a stove. Have to go to Hams Fork Station before we can get water, making our distance traveled today 32 miles. Only 33 miles farther to Fort

Most of the emigrants' inscriptions along the Overland Trail date to the 1860s.

(Top) The Point of Rocks Stage Station was first built in 1862 or 1863 to serve the Overland Stageline.

(Bottom) The Hallville Mine was short-lived. In 1868, when production was at its peak, the town boasted the finest restaurant west of Cheyenne. True or false, the advertisements for the Hallville restaurant point out that in 1868, restaurants, a coal mine, and several homes were located at this town built along the main line of the Union Pacific Railroad. The small structure shown here now blends into the sandstone ridge on which it was constructed.

Bridger. Shall strike the route to California via Ft. Laramie and South Pass tomorrow. Can see the Telegraph Poles from our camp. A large number of wagons camped near us tonight. Bureau Co. train, a train of 7 wagons loaded with merchandise for Salt Lake City, wagons and merchandise to be sold there, and the Mules taking things to California. Our train of 8 wagons, and another train of 8 or 10 wagons. In the evening all hands join in a grand dance in the station. Our roads nearly level all day and very dusty and in some places sandy. Game in sight of a range of snow capped mountains, after gaining the top of bluffs on Green River. The weather since entering the mountains has been uniformly even, always pleasant, very warm at noon, very cold at sunrise, and cold all night. Always a good breeze. Miner took in a man today that was hustler at Black Butte Station, he followed us in the Coach. The country begins to improve a little do see some thing beside the everlasting wild sage. Wood very scarce, have seen no timber with the exception of a few pine shrub on the side of Mountains a long way off.

June 11th. Have a great time recovering our horses and mules from an Island where we put them last night for grass. Would drive them all down the bank and get a dozen or so fairly in the

water and think they would all follow across, but after going a few rods they would suddenly wheel and put back to the Island again, leading us a wild chase after them. Finally have to lead them across two or three at a time. We enter the old California road about 9 1/2 o'clock, stop for dinner on the bank of the Black Fork at Church Buttes Station. Ford the Black Fork again, and soon after found another stream running into the Black Fork. Hooper crossing first did not take the right track, struck deep water and wet his wagon bed. Both rivers about 50 yards wide. Camped for the night within two miles of Millerville Station, traveled 10 miles today and arrive in Camp early, when all hands go in bathing. The roads very good and level today in the valley of Black Fork, but dreadful dusty, a regular bed of ashes. Very hot day should have been pleased to have a little of the snow from a range of mountains ahead of us where tops are covered with it. . . .[44]

Hallville, built in 1868, enjoyed a brief life while it housed a small group of coal miners attempting to make a living along the Union Pacific Railroad. This building is all that remains of a small house at Hallville.

Cutting was not alone in denigrating the water in Bitter Creek. He was also not the only one to appreciate the beauty of Green River and the sandstone that outcropped along the trail. Dr. Waid Howard, who traveled along the Bitter Creek Valley in 1865, claimed "after nine long days and nights spent upon what is called the Bitter Creek Desert . . . we finally succeeded in reaching the banks of the long sought and delightful stream Green River."[45] In spite of the dust and alkali water, most emigrants found the rock formations along Bitter Creek inspiring. Dr. Howard, in describing the trip west from Point of Rocks to the river, wrote, "For many miles the mountains have appeared to rise higher and higher and seem to be closing in upon us as it were, until we look upon them in their mystic grandeur, surmounted by butte after butte, with awe and astonishment."[46] Within three short years the valley described by Dr. Howard would be crossed by the first transcontinental railroad.

Chapter II
THE TOWN BUILDERS
1868-1917

Early in 1868, railroad grading crews were stretched along the length of Sweetwater County. By the end of 1868, railroad rails had been laid across the county and the territory of Wyoming was a reality. Created in 1868, this new territory began with five counties: Albany, Laramie, Carbon, Sweetwater, and Uinta. They were all border-to-border counties; they owed their existence to the railroad. Eventually, they would shrink to their present size, but in 1868, they were long large counties occupied by few people.

Not only did new counties emerge in 1868, but towns grew up along parallel ribbons of steel being laid in a westerly direction at record speeds. From Cheyenne to the Utah border, daily the tracks pushed westward. In one year, 1868, the tracks crossed not only the mountains of Wyoming, but the entire state.

As graders, then track layers, reached Sweetwater County, towns or villages sprang up to serve the needs of the laborers. Merchants, bartenders, newspapermen, blacksmiths, miners, and railroad repairmen began to arrive in increasing numbers. Boom towns like Bitter Creek, Hallville, Point of Rocks, Green River, and Bryan sprang up overnight. Rock Springs grew from a small coal mining venture run by Archibald and Duncan Blair. These two brothers opened a mine near what was destined to become the largest mining town in the area. The county seat lay to the north in a gold mining camp that grew by leaps and bounds. The town, called South Pass, was located north of the Oregon Trail and was situated along a stream bearing gold nuggets and gold dust. South Pass would remain the seat of Sweetwater County until the citizens of Green River City literally and figuratively "stole" the county seat. Of course, an election to move the county seat was held and Green River won, but South Pass refused to send the records to the town along the railroad tracks. According to legend, men from Green River ultimately seized

Rock Springs city officials on December 2, 1893; on the lower left is John Hartney, on the upper left (to right) is Morgan Griffith and Edward Thorpe; the others are unidentified.

the records in order to gain possession.[1] Unhappy, South Pass residents later became part of Fremont County. Not only did South Pass City, Miner's Delight, and Atlantic City eventually become part of Fremont County, but so did the Sweetwater River. Sweetwater County is named for this river in Fremont County, but political battles of the last century deprived Sweetwater County of the watercourse for which it was named.

The building of the Union Pacific Railroad (UPRR) created Sweetwater County. This is true not in the sense that UPRR measured the boundaries or laid out the county lines, but because the railroad roundhouses at Bryan and Bitter Creek and the coal mines at Hallville, Point of Rocks, and Rock Springs owed their existence to the railroad. Bridge builders, and later yardmen in Green River City, were also all employed by the railroad. The construction and maintenance of the railroad caused Sweetwater County to come into existence.

In 1868, a boom of major proportions spread across southern Wyoming. Thousands of workers scraped and cut level grades and laid tracks. Into towns like Green River City they came seeking whiskey, wine, or whatever else they could find to divert their attention from the fast-paced westward push across the territory. Green River,

View of camp at Black Buttes, the last station of the Union Pacific Railroad on the Red Desert, September 1868. Drawing by a Frenchman named A. Marie, after a sketch he made at the site. Courtesy of the Union Pacific Railroad Museum, Omaha.

merely a stage station and ferry landing a few years earlier, became a tent city that boasted a newspaper, hotels, and numerous other buildings. The newspaper editor was the irrepressible Leigh Freeman.

Leigh Freeman was renowned for his free opinion and biting criticism of nearly everything and everyone. Ultimately, he seemed to turn friendships into bitter battles of words and poured forth rivers of ink to avenge any perceived slight. Numerous people commented on his "bold and fearless" writing style.[2] Others criticized his lack of restraint and endless speeches. The Crow Indians called him "Big Jaw" because he talked all the time.[3] Supposedly, a Lt. John B. Suray conducted a fake funeral and wrote a mock epitaph for Freeman in 1866 that proclaimed: "Here lie the remains of Leigh R. Freeman/He lived and died a printer's demon/Stranger, tread lightly on this sod/For if he gapes, your gone."[4] In August 1868, this prolific talker, writer, and editor arrived on the banks of the Green River.[5] He stayed until late fall 1868, when he took his press to Bear River City near present Evanston, Wyoming.

Leigh was accompanied by his brother, Frederick. Together they managed the *Frontier Index,* the "Press on Wheels" and provided insights into the color and excitement of freighting over the Overland Trail in 1868. Stagecoaches traveling along the Overland Trail in 1868 were numerous and laden with mail, fast freight, and passengers. Stages conveyed the *Frontier Index* "to all the grading and mining camps." Passengers on westbound stages took supper in Green River City as did eastbound coaches.[6] As the railroad progressed closer to Green River, "Passengers over the Union Pacific Railroad [were] transferred to and from the stages at Point of Rocks."[7]

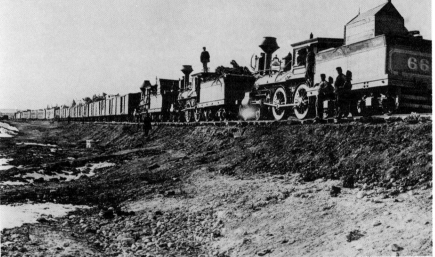

(Top) Carmichael's grading crews on Bitter Creek. "Carmichael, a grading subcontractor, had a difficult job of cut and fill throughout Wyoming. The hills had to be cut down and the Valley's filled in. Fills were built from both sides of the valley at once as this picture shows." A. J. Russell photograph, Courtesy of the Union Pacific Railroad Museum, Omaha.

(Bottom) "Construction train employed by Casement Brothers" in 1868. Used in building the Union Pacific Railroad. "The workers lived in and on top of the long cars." A. J. Russell photograph, Courtesy of the Union Pacific Railroad Museum, Omaha.

(Top) Carmichael's Camp east of Green River was a typical graders' camp. This photograph, taken in 1868, shows the Overland Trail in the foreground and the telegraph line. Courtesy of the Union Pacific Railroad Museum, Omaha.

(Bottom) Carmichael's Cut made by the graders at Carmichael's Camp in 1868.

With the numerous stagecoaches traveling the trail alongside freighters and emigrants, accidents were bound to happen. On October 13, 1868, "one of Wells, Fargo and Co.'s stages upset within twenty steps" of Leigh Freeman's "sleeping apartment" in Green River City. Freeman, ever prone to avenge even the smallest slight, proclaimed: "This upsetting [of] stages has become such a provoking and dangerous nuisance that the public are [sic] availing themselves of any and all other means of travel, rather than risk their limbs and lives with Wells, Fargo & Co."[8] Previously the editor of the traveling newspaper had reported that "we are sorry to meet our old and esteemed plains freighter, Mr. Alexander Majors, in a crippled condition, from the stage upsetting a few miles from here." Freeman went on to complain, "Stage upsetting in this vicinity is getting to be such an aggravated nuisance that persons are taking bull teams in preference to risking their limbs and lives in Concord coaches."[9]

Numerous stagecoaches ran short routes between grading camps, end-of-track towns, and places like Green River City. Apparently following the Overland Trail west, a stage line served the budding town of Bryan in the fall of 1868. The "Bryan Express," as it was called, was managed by N. E. Kellog. "Covered spring carriages with fast teams" left the Jenks House in Green River bound west for

Bryan "every morning at nine o'clock." From "Martin's" in Bryan a similar coach headed east to Green River at 9:00 A.M. "carrying passengers and light packages. Fare for round trip, five dollars."[10] The Bryan Express provided a much needed service for those hoping to travel only a short distance.

The stagecoaches passing through the Bitter Creek Valley were not immune to robbery. In August 1868, several thousand dollars ("principally gold dust and bullion") were stolen in a hold-up of a Wells, Fargo stagecoach. "There were no passengers on the coach except a stage company blacksmith." Taking the strongbox a short distance from the coach, the thieves removed the valuables then "took to the hills leaving the box and remains of letter and etc., in the sagebrush." A reward of fifteen thousand dollars was offered for the return of the treasure and "capture and conviction of the robbers." Of course, the robbers could be returned dead or alive.[11]

The presence of Native Americans anywhere along the tracks or near the Overland Trail sparked interest throughout the territory of Wyoming. Leigh Freeman repeatedly reported the location of Shoshonis, Utes, and Sioux Indians. Shoshonis visited Bear River City in November, where they traded for necessary goods.[12] Freeman, whose motto was "only White Men to be naturalized citizens," warned the inhabitants of Bear River City: "Persons should be careful about allowing liquor to pass into the hands of these Lamanite brethren [i.e. Native Americans] as there is a fine of $300 and imprisonment for trading them liquor or ammunition."[13] Quick to point out any alleged "depredation," Freeman reported that "The Indians killed and scalped two white men near Sulphur Springs" in June. Apparently this incident happened some-

Camp Carmichael just east of Green River in 1868. A. J. Russell photograph, Courtesy of the Union Pacific Railroad Museum, Omaha.

This photograph was taken on what is now Black Butte's coal lease sometime in the 1860s. Courtesy of the Union Pacific Railroad Museum Collection, Omaha.

Rock Springs prior to 1890. This photograph was taken facing south.

where near Sulphur Springs stage station. Numerous "sightings" of Sioux and Shoshoni Indians were reported, but given the number of people traveling east and west through southern Wyoming in 1868, there was a minimal number of armed conflicts between Euro-Americans and Native Americans along the future railroad route in Sweetwater County.[14] The noted exception to this took place near Fort LaClede, where both railroad surveyors and Indians were killed in a pitched battle.[15] While it is difficult to obtain comparative statistics, based on Freeman's newspaper, you were more likely to be killed by a bullet in an "end of track town" than by an arrow from a warrior's bow.

The stagecoaches continued to run from the end of tracks to points further west, but as the railroad neared Green River, the distance that mail and freight had to travel was shortened. Green River began to emerge as a vibrant community. Since a bridge had to be built across the river, workers congregated at the Green River. In 1868, three ferries operated, carrying freight, wagons, and men across the river.[16] The newly-constructed town was teeming with activity. "The streets were crowded with wagons loaded with every variety of merchandise."[17] About five miles east of Green River was Carmichael's graders' camp. Near present-day Rock Springs, a coal mine was opened.[18] The Bitter Creek Valley from Rock Springs to Green River now had hundreds of residents.

In June 1868, Green River was called a "Little Town." By July it was referred to as Green River City.[19] Leigh Freeman in his July 3 edition reported, "On a bottom about one mile wide, surrounded by picturesque bluffs, we found some five hundred people [living] in tents, portable buildings and adobe houses; and many hundreds pouring in from Salt Lake, South Pass and North Platte."[20] Green River City was beginning to expand. Soon it would become an "end-of-the-tracks town," with saloons, gaming houses, and the associated vices common to railroad towns across the territory. Most end-of-the-tracks towns were just that, the point where the rails ended. End-of-the-tracks town, however, is something of a misnomer; it did not mean the tracks ended at that point. Instead, it was a location where freight and supplies were stored for shipment further down the line. Towns were built at spots along the line where more work was required to insure the railroad construction went smoothly. In the case of Green River City, the river served as an obstacle to the progress of the railroad. As a result, the completion of the railroad had to await the completion of the bridge. This work was done in advance of the rail line, allowing the locomotives to cross the river once the rails reached the bridge. To continue west, goods had to be stockpiled along the banks of the Green River awaiting the ferry ride across the water. In Wyoming, Cheyenne, Laramie, and Benton preceded Green River as important supply points. During the late summer and early fall of 1868, however, Green River was the scene of major activity. It had everything needed by a railroader, including Leigh Freeman's "Newspaper on Wheels," the *Frontier Index.*

Towns such as Green River were bustling enterprises. On September 22, 1868, it was reported, "The tide of business at Green has been heavier, higher and more monied during the past few days than ever before." The streets were crowded with loaded wagons containing all types of merchandise. "The Jenks House, Star, U.S. and Lyon's restaurants . . . feed about twelve hundred people each day, and besides these are a dozen chop houses."[21] Green River now was a town of over one thousand people. Most of the occupants were

men. Towns such as Green River were notorious for their nightlife. At Kingston's Dance Hall, on a hot August evening, a fight broke out and during the melee a revolver was fired, sending a bullet "through the top of the tent." The man with the revolver was arrested and the other brawler had his wounds dressed by a doctor in town.[22]

The Freeman brothers often found themselves near or in

(Top) Photograph of Green River Station 1868-1869. (A. J. Russel Photograph, Courtesy Wyoming State Archives, Museums, and Historical Department; much of the A. J. Russell Collection is at the Oakland Museum or Union Pacific Railroad Museum, Omaha)

(Bottom) From this office the coal mines at Rock Springs were run like clockwork.

trouble and complained about the nocturnal habits of some of the Green River residents. Freeman reported on September 29: "A bullet came within a few feet of our writing table last night, so close that we dodged. It came from the revolver of Jack O'Neil in the neighborhood of the Star Restaurant, on Green street, thus passing entirely through two rows of occupied buildings, and in its heedless course might have killed or wounded one or more persons." "Five other shots," Freeman adds, "were fired about the same time in the same random manner, the reports which rallied a large crowd, eager to see who was so lucky as to have been sent to the Happy Hunting Grounds of his fore-fathers this time." In typical Freeman style, he began to editorialize, writing: "O'Neil was arrested and fined, though not half enough for such an offense. Hereafter any one who so far violates the city ordinance and respect for himself and the community by creating such alarms and endangering the lives of the people, should be banished from the elysian corporation of Green River to inhale the fumes of brimstone and drink molten lava at the Devil's Well in the fiery regions of Yellowstone Lake."[23] While Green River was quick to pass an ordinance against discharging firearms within the town limits, enforcing the law was quite a different matter.

Leigh Freeman, like many others before and after him, found the bluffs surrounding Green River remarkably attractive and noted that in the fall of 1868, an

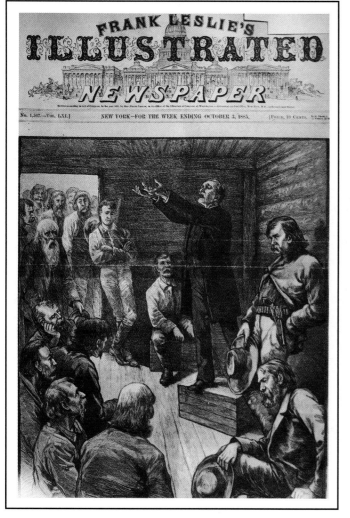

artist came to town to paint the "palisades" north of Green River. He reports, "Mr. G. W. Platt, the noted artist of the U.P.R.R. towns is at Green River, painting landscape views of the bluffs, mountains, river islands and Nature's towers. His painting of the grand old cliffs, overhanging the river just above the railroad, together with the island and the river, is one of remarkable attractiveness."[24] The island mentioned by Freemen is currently called Expedition Island. It became the starting point for John Wesley Powell's 1869 expedition down the Green and Colorado Rivers. A. J. Russell, Union Pacific photographer, would photograph the palisades as did William Henry Jackson, the famous photographer who accompanied Ferdinand Hayden's geological expeditions through Wyoming. The palisades, the Green River islands, and the canyon walls have been the subject of artists and photographers since 1868.

On October 9, 1868, the bridge across the Green River was completed. Four days later, the rails extended to Bryan. In a few more days the tracks exited Sweetwater County. In its wake, the railroad left small towns at Bitter Creek, Point of Rocks, Hallville, Rock Springs, Green River, and Bryan. Only Rock Springs and Green River survive to this day. Only Point of Rocks remains a charming testimony to the passing trains and stagecoaches of the 1860s. At Point of Rocks, a sandstone stage station built by Ben Holladay's Stage Company and wood railroad section houses built by Union Pacific Railroad still stand.

With the railroad built, Sweetwater County entered a settling-in phase. Union Pacific had to develop the resources along its tracks if it wanted to remain afloat financially. Mining coal along the mainline required many men, hence, towns emerged alongside the mines. Places like

This pamphlet condemned Territorial Governor F. E. Warren for using federal troops to return Chinese miners to Rock Springs after the September 2, 1885 Chinese Massacre. (Courtesy American Heritage Center, University of Wyoming)

⬦ F. E. WARREN, THE CHINESE PROTECTOR. ⬦

⬦ "PACK THE JURY, THEY MUST BE CONVICTED." ⬦

No white miner can afford to vote for Warren and his Chinese record.

"Guilty, or not guilty, they must be convicted."

He believes in protecting American labor. See other side.

"More soldiers and bayonets, my friends the Chinese must be protected."

He is peculiar for ways that are dark and tricks that are vain.

"I propose to keep the Chinese here and if you make any further trouble with them, I'll leave a hole in the ground where Almy now stands."

If he can't keep his Chinese friends in the mines, he is going to employ them to old down his fraudulent pre-emption claims.

Chinese New Year parade in Rock Springs in 1896.

An 1896 Chinese parade in Rock Springs. The flags are the "Stars and Stripes" and a Manchurian banner.

Rock Springs were transformed from stage stations to towns. The coal mines and the railroad created an urban frontier where towns were built before almost anything else.

The railroad required coal to fuel the locomotives traveling east and west along the mainline built in 1868. Initially, the mines were operated by Thomas Wardell, who was under contract to Union Pacific to provide coal for the railroad. By 1874, Union Pacific assumed control of the mines in Sweetwater County. In the decade of the 1870s, Union Pacific was the leading employer in the county. Most people worked for either the railroad or the coal company. Businesses were built to serve Union Pacific employees and the few ranches scattered around the county. But in the 1870s, most people lived in towns or communities built for the purpose of serving Union Pacific's needs and the primary need was coal.

The presence of coal in the area was first reported by Howard Stansbury in 1850. It was in this year that Stansbury passed through the Bitter Creek Valley on the way east. Near present Rock Springs, Stansbury noted "a bed of bituminous coal cropping out of the north bluff of the valley with every indication of its being quite abundant."[25] He also noted coal outcrops in the vicinity of present-day Point of Rocks. In 1865 James Evans, who was responsible for surveying the proposed Union Pacific rail line, presented a more detailed report of the coal resources found in the area. South of Point of Rocks, he noted that coal mining was taking place adjacent to a stage station and stated, "At Black Butte, 30 miles from the summit of Bitter Creek and on our line, where this coal occurs, several seams have been opened, one 5 feet, and one 3 1/2 feet of clean coal. . . . This is the hardest and best quality of coal found on the line."[26] Coal used in Overland Stage stations was also mined at Rock Springs.

With the arrival of the Union Pacific Railroad in 1868, coal mining began in earnest in the Bitter Creek Valley. The Blair brothers, Archibald and Duncan, who at one time ran the stage station at Rock Springs, opened a mine south of Bitter Creek in 1868. Some sources suggest that the Blairs actually began mining coal in 1867, but with the arrival of the railroad, the success of their coal mining ventures was assured. The *Frontier Index* gave a brief mention to the presence of the mines at present-day Rock Springs in 1868. The paper reported: "There is a big coal mine opened twenty miles above here, within fifty yards of the track, and the accommodating R.R.Co. is putting in a side track there. Quit your shivering and patronize the coal miners and adobe makers."[27]

By 1870 a number of coal mines operated along the Bitter Creek Valley. These include the mines at Rock Springs, Black Butte, the "Van Dyk" mine (after 1908 the spelling changes to Van Dyke), the Blair mine, the Point of Rocks mine, and the mine at "Hall" (Hallville). Hallville was located adjacent to the Union Pacific mainline south of present Point of Rocks. The Van Dyk mine was located about four miles east of Rock Springs and in 1870, produced fifty tons daily. Clarence King, who was commissioned to conduct a geological survey of the fortieth parallel for the United States government, stated, "The coal from this mine is considered, and is proved by analysis, to be the best hitherto found along the line of the railroad."[28]

The mines in the Bitter Creek Valley soon began to draw statewide attention. A report by the surveyor general of Wyoming Territory, Silas Reed, gives an excellent description of the "Bitter Creek Valley" coal mines. He writes: "Work was commenced in November, 1868, at the Rock Springs No. 1 Mine. The company now employs 85 men at this mine. This thickness of the coal is 10 feet." Reed contends that during the year 1870, "No. 1" produced 21,109 tons of coal, and the total tonnage from November 1868 to December 31, 1870, was 38,308. He notes that of this amount, "35,359

Archaeological excavations in China Town (1991) showing artifacts found above one of the floors in the houses that were uncovered. These houses were occupied by Chinese workers in Rock Springs. Courtesy of the Archaeological Services, Western Wyoming College.

tons were consumed by the Union Pacific Railroad, and 2,949 were shipped to private parties." The surveyor general reported that several other mines were in operation in Sweetwater County including: "Van Dyk and Hallville on the border of the railroad. . . . They are owned by capitalists in San Francisco, though not extensively worked now."[29] The article goes on to extol the virtue of Rock Springs coal and claimed it to be "literally inexhaustible." In describing its qualities, Reed writes: "It is superior to all other coal in this region for domestic and mechanical purposes. . . . For blacksmiths' use, it has superseded charcoal, both in Wyoming and Colorado, and is the only coal used in this Territory by blacksmiths."[30]

Coal production rapidly increased in Wyoming Territory. The bulk of this production came from Sweetwater County. With each increase in coal production came the corresponding need to hire more men. More men require additional housing and services and with each expansion of the coal industry, Rock Springs grew. In 1868 the mines along the Union Pacific Railroad produced 6,925 tons of coal. By 1875 this amount had climbed to 208,222 tons, and in 1880, the output reached 527,811 tons.[31] Initially, the mining was done by the Wyoming Coal and Mining Company, which was under contract to the railroad. The federal government criticized this arrangement, claiming profits were too high; since the government had underwritten the construction of the railroad, in the form of generous loans and land grants, the government's concerns were viewed seriously. But even more important than government's concerns was Union Pacific's desire to

Chinese New Year parade in Rock Springs. Courtesy American Heritage Center, University of Wyoming, Neg. #20424, photograph not dated.

Chinese New Year parade is shown traveling through Chinatown (not dated).

gain more of the profits from its coal mining ventures. The contract with Wyoming Coal and Mining Company was terminated in 1874 and the Union Pacific took direct control of their own mining operations. As T. A. Larson, a noted Wyoming historian, observes: "No doubt the Union Pacific profited handsomely from its coal, using it as fuel, selling it at high prices, and charging outrageous freight rates."[32] The value of the coal mines to the Union Pacific cannot be overestimated. In fact, Union Pacific president Charles Francis Adams, Jr., testified in 1887 that coal mines were "the salvation of the Union Pacific; these mines saved it. Otherwise, the Union Pacific would not have been worth picking up."[33]

When Union Pacific formed its coal company in 1874, it almost immediately became the dominate force in the Wyoming coal industry. In many ways, until the Interstate Commerce Commission (ICC) moved against Union Pacific at the Black Butte Mine in Sweetwater County in the early 1900s, Union Pacific enjoyed a virtual coal mining monopoly in Sweetwater County. The monopoly was easily maintained because all coal had to be shipped over the Union Pacific Railroad. With the exception of the Blairtown mine and a few other small mines, the coal mines in Sweetwater County were controlled by the Union Pacific. This total domination lasted until the latter decades of the nineteenth century when Patrick J. Quealy began his mining ventures south of town. This fact is clearly seen in 1889, when the secretary of the territory compiled a publication on "The Vacant Public Lands and How to Obtain Them." In this publication, the secretary notes that in Rock Springs, there were eight producing coal mines, five of which were owned by Union Pacific.[34] Union Pacific controlled more than just the railroad.

A report issued by the Wyoming territorial geologist in 1890

This 1894 photograph portrays the arrest of "Coxey's Army" in Green River. According to T. A. Larson, General Jacob S. Coxey, a Populist who called for a march on Washington to generate support for public works projects, led "Coxey's Army" as the group commandeered trains in the West and passed through Wyoming in April and May of 1894 enroute to Washington. In May of 1894, U. S. Marshal Joseph P. Rankin arrested fifteen leaders in Green River. Four companies of troops from Fort D. A. Russel took charge of the leaders based on an appeal made by Rankin.

Colonel Callahan and Green River Mayor Taliaferro before the arrest of Coxey's Army on May 15, 1894.

Rock Springs at about 1890. College Hill and White Mountain are visible in the background.

H. R. Kuy Kendall stagecoach in Rock Springs (1890s). This stageline served Rock Springs and Lander for a brief time in the late 1890s. Courtesy of the Denver Public Library.

presents a more detailed discussion of mining operations in Sweetwater County. According to Louis D. Ricketts (territorial geologist) during the years 1888 and 1889 the Union Pacific Coal Company operated six mines in Rock Springs. These mines included No. 1, No. 3, No. 4, No. 5, No. 7, and No. 8. At the time, independent firms ran the Van Dyk, Rock Springs Coal Company No. 1 and No. 2, and the Hopkins Mine.[35] The Rock Springs Coal Company mines were operated by P. J. Quealy, who would eventually open the Kemmerer Coal Company mines at present-day Lincoln County, Wyoming. The state geologist went on to say that ten mines were open and operating during the period from 1888 to 1889. Conversely, the secretary of the territory for the year 1889 mentions only eight. This is partially explained by the fact that two of these mines were not opened until late 1889. Because they did not operate until late 1889, the secretary of the territory might simply have overlooked the mines or issued the report too early in the year to have been aware of their existence. Moreover, there is some conflicting information in the territorial geologist's report regarding the actual operating condition of the Union Pacific No. 8 mine.[36]

The fact that Rock Springs owes its existence to the coal mines is clearly seen in the early reports and descriptions of the town. An 1889 description proclaimed, "Fourteen miles east of Green River City are located the celebrated Rock Springs coal mines, the annual output of which is worth over $3,000,000 and is likely to be doubled within the next two years."[37] The report goes on to describe the town, stating: "Rock Springs is a busy, thriving mining city of over 3,000 inhabitants in the center of the best coal producing country in the Rocky Mountains. This place was first settled on the building of the railroad in [1868]. In 1877 it figured as a small mining camp of 450 people, but since 1885 it has undergone a growth that has more than doubled its population and brought to it the advantage arising from a regularly incorporated municipality, with an enterprise similar to an eastern metropolis."[38]

By 1889, numerous improvements were evident in Rock Springs. They included: "a $250,000 system of water works, the streets and buildings are lighted with arc and incandescent lights, four churches, two schools, a bank, a volunteer fire department, two weekly newspapers, several hotels, and excellent commercial houses."[39] Although Rock Springs did not equal many of the gold and silver camps in nearby Colorado or Montana in wealth and size, it possessed qualities similar to other nineteenth-century mining camps. And by coal mining town standards, Rock Springs was a substantial settlement in 1889. However, in the years from 1868 to 1885, more attention was focused on Green River than on the dusty coal town along Bitter Creek.

An 1877 traveler on a westward-bound train gave a unique tourist's view of Sweetwater County from the window of his railroad car. "The stations along the route slip away," the traveler wrote,

"Rock Springs in the 1870s" is the caption assigned this photograph which shows the Beckwith and Quinn store at the time.

This November 1898 photograph shows, from left to right, Mrs. Thomas, Lloyd Thomas, Emily Anderson, and Gus Anderson. Early family photographs from either Rock Springs or Green River are a rarity.

"and leave no other impression behind than of a brown dot in a vast space."[40] The train rushed "through a narrow, rocky ravine into Bitter Creek Valley, passing the little stream that winds through it, brackish and undrinkable as Dead Sea water." Like many people, the tourist was taken by the rock formations when "mile after mile of bluffs, sharp curves, and long ranks of buttes, thick with grotesque carvings and delicate tracery; solitary lights in lonely little telegraph houses; tall, columnlike boulders at Points of Rocks and a few scattered houses, remnants of what was once a fast little town before it gave up the ghost."[41] The unnamed tourist never mentioned Rock Springs, noting that: "As the sun rises for the fourth time since we left Omaha, we roll, rejoicing into the Green River Valley."[42]

At Green River City, the tourist noted there was snow on the ground. "The snow lies white and deep in every hollow" but the sun was "out dazzlingly." As the train departed the station headed west towards the Green River he noted: "The early sunlight blazes on the snow and the deep rich red of the rocks, and the rippling green water, and overhead the sky is blue—such a blue! Every man longs to be a painter, but what painter could copy all this upon which the sun shines every day?"[43] This was the tourist's last report on what he saw in Sweetwater County. His next entry described the town of Piedmont in Uinta County.

In 1870 there were 117 people in the small town of Rock Springs. By 1880 the population had increased to 763 residents, and 3,406 people were living there by 1890. This growth came with the development of the Union Pacific Coal Company, but it was not accomplished without tension.[44] Many of these residents were immigrants from Europe and Asia who came seeking employment in the coal mines.

Even by 1870 the county was extremely diversified. The county ran from Utah to Montana, but in the area that came to be present Sweetwater County, the diversity was great. At Point of Rocks, for example, in 1870, there were sixty-five residents. This included three Scotchmen, six Irishmen, four Englishmen, one Canadian and one Bavarian, all male. There were also female emigrants, five Irish women and three from England. What is most intriguing is that Caroline Dill, age forty-two, who was born and raised in England, served as justice of the peace of Point of Rocks in 1870. Her husband, Robert, also born in England, was the railroad clerk.[45] To the south of Point of Rocks at Hallville, there were twenty-four residents. Of that number, only five were born in the United States. The rest came from Ireland, Wales, Scotland, England, Prussia, and China.[46] Most had traveled to their new homes by train.

(Top) This photograph was taken by Reverend R. H. Smith who "missionized" Rock Springs Chinatown in 1896. Photograph depicts Chinese homes at the time.

(Bottom) Fire at the Miners' Hospital in Rock Springs, January 4, 1897. The building was gutted and had to be replaced with the General Hospital.

(Top) Beckwith and Quinn Company in Rock Springs photographed between 1890 and 1900.

(Bottom) This home made from stone was built sometime in the late 1800s. It was located in Rock Springs.

Emigrants moving to Sweetwater County to work in the mines or on the railroad most often arrived by train. Transported by railroad cars from New York City or San Francisco, Europeans and Asians moved to the interior of the Rocky Mountains seeking opportunities. While we do not know how long they stayed in coastal cities like New York or Philadelphia, we do have a brief glimpse of what life was like in a railroad car for emigrants.

In 1877, Mrs. Frank Leslie took a pleasure trip from "Gotham to the Golden Gate." Her trip spanned the months of April and June and this remarkable traveler noted many people and places she witnessed along the way. Traveling from New York City to San Francisco in a Pullman Car, she took her trip west in style. Yet she was aware of the traveling conditions of others. On her return trip, Mrs. Leslie got off the train at Green River. A twenty-minute "lay-over" allowed her to view two "newly-caught [mountain] lions, romping and snarling in their cages on the platform." Upon reboarding she left her berth to visit editors from Nebraska in another railroad car. "In order to do so," Mrs. Leslie writes, we had "to pass through two or three sleeping cars closely packed, and an emigrant car where, by the dull light, we could see the poor creatures curled and huddled up in heaps for the night, with no possibility of lying down comfortably; but men, women, bundles, baskets and babies, in one promiscuous heap."[47] In Victorian society, everything that involved touching could be labeled promiscuous. Yet what Mrs. Leslie described is the scene of a railroad car packed with emigrants bound eastward.[48] She was headed back to New York. Only speculation can fill in the gaps left out by her description, but the fact that she even noted emigrants traveling eastward suggests that they were probably Asians or returning settlers from California, Nevada, Utah, or even western Wyoming. Many such travelers were headed east to seek opportunities or to return to their former homes.

When the Union Pacific took over the coal company in 1874 it initiated several changes. Principal among these changes was the choice to hire Chinese miners in Rock Springs. Jay Gould, noted business baron and entrepreneur, was in control of the Union Pacific. Gould, after 1874, took steps to reduce the cost of coal. Since Union Pacific owned the coal, it seemed the simplest way to reduce the cost of coal production was to reduce labor costs. Using Chinese miners proved to be the most successful means to accomplish this goal. Unfortunately, miners of other nationalities resented the fact that Union Pacific cut wages; and when white miners complained, Chinese miners took their places. Misunderstandings and mutual suspicion eventually led to racial tension between white miners and Chinese workers. The term "white miners" was applied to all non-Chinese workers. These white miners saw the Chinese miners as the source of their problems.[49]

On September 2, 1885, more Chinese lived in the town of Rock Springs than any other nationality. On the second day of the month, white miners, who were in the minority, attacked and burned Chinatown. The tragedy centered around a labor dispute that came to a head on this September day. When the smoke settled, twenty-eight Chinese miners were dead. The charred remnants of Chinese homes marked the north side of Rock Springs.

The impact of the Chinese Massacre affected the town of Rock Springs for years to come. Almost half of the town was in ashes. Chinatown would have to be rebuilt. Union Pacific, while saying they would never give in to the demands of labor organizers, would have to change its policies. The Chinese Massacre jolted the Union Pacific. Although Chinese miners were still valued by the coal company, several factors combined to alter the hiring practices of the coal company. First, recently passed federal laws restricted the

The palisades at Green River. This picture is from an early twentieth-century Sweetwater County telephone book.

number of Chinese who could emigrate to the United States. This resulted in fewer Chinese workers available to seek employment. Secondly, Union Pacific began to mechanize its mines and thus reduce the number of people needed to remove the coal. Finally, Union Pacific Coal Company would never again concentrate on hiring just one nationality. Its policy shifted towards hiring miners from many different countries. Employing miners from around the world prevented one group from dominating the industry and also prevented labor unions from forming. The result was that Rock Springs became a city made up of citizens from around the world.[50]

The task of recording the changes that Rock Springs underwent during the 1880s fell to newspapers, photographers, and a variety of writers

Joseph E. Stimpson photographed the Green River Sodaworks in the early 1900s. Courtesy of the Wyoming State Archives, Museums and Historical Department, Cheyenne.

The sheriff in this Green River Saloon was known as Constable Frank Kidd (photograph undated).

keeping official documents for the federal government and for the Union Pacific Railroad. Photographs from the mid-1880s abound due to the historic events surrounding the Chinese Massacre. The pictures focus on the Chinese return to Rock Springs in late September 1885, and the arrival of the U.S. Army and the officials who came to investigate the tragic events of September 2. These pictures, along with photographs taken by Union Pacific for its corporate records, provide a point of comparison for future generations of Rock Springs historians. They are a benchmark by which to gauge the changes that have occurred since the mid-1880s. The photographs illustrate the diverse composition of the people living in the town at the time.[51]

In 1890, when Wyoming became a state, it was obvious even to visitors that Rock Springs depended on a particular commodity for its economic well-being. Coal dust covered homes and miners alike. Mining and the railroad were the only industries in town, and these industries were controlled by the Union Pacific. The effects of Union Pacific's policies of hiring diverse ethnic groups was readily apparent in 1890. Finnish, English, Scotch, Chinese, and Irish miners were reported to be working in the coal mines of Rock Springs during the 1890s.[52]

In 1891, the Union Pacific Passenger Department, whose goal was to attract people to settle in Wyoming, also presented glowing reports of Rock Springs and the associated coal mines. In their 1891 pamphlet for the "Home Seeker, Capitalist and Tourist," Union Pacific claimed: "Perhaps no other city or town in Wyoming is increasing in population, wealth, and general importance as rapidly as Rock Springs. Though situated in the much abased Bitter Creek region, it is destined to become one of the large centers of population." By 1891, coal mining employed "over 1,500 men and this number will be more than doubled in the not distant future."[53] The article also claims that in 1891, three thousand people lived in Rock Springs. Taken that fifteen hundred men were employed in the mines, this shows that half the population was involved in mining.[54] Other than coal mining, there were few forms of employment open to people settling in Sweetwater County during the latter

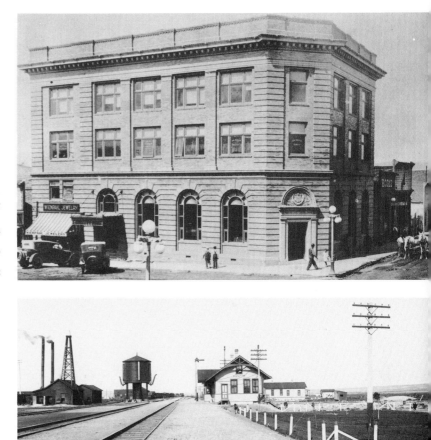

(Top) North Side State Bank and North Front Street, early 1900s.

(Bottom) Wamsutter's Depot near the turn of the century. Courtesy Wyoming State Archives, Museums and Historical Department, Cheyenne.

(Top) This photograph in Rock Springs dates to near the turn of the century.

(Bottom) North Front Street, Rock Springs, early 1900s. The Oxford is "supposedly the saloon Butch Cassidy hid in before leaving for South America."

half of the nineteenth century. While ranching offered some opportunities in the late 1800s, the coal mines and the railroad employed the largest number of workers.

Not surprisingly, Union Pacific was the dominant force in the settlement and growth of Rock Springs. Dyer Clark, Union Pacific's driving force in the Wyoming coal fields, told his supervisors in a 1900 letter why he hired so many immigrants to work in the Rock Springs mines. Clark wrote to his supervisors in Omaha, "Every possible care is taken to keep nationalities mixed, and not allow any nationality to predominate . . . ." According to Clark, the purpose of keeping the nationalities mixed was to discourage the growth of labor unions. Union Pacific Coal Company was growing, and it felt labor unions would slow its growth. And as the coal company grew, so did the town of Rock Springs.[55]

At the turn of the century, new mines were opened at Rock Springs and the town witnessed the development of new businesses. The town was expanding, and photographers recorded this expansion. Not only was Rock Springs growing, but so was Green River. In 1903, Joseph E. Stimpson took photographs of many towns along the Union Pacific's route. Stimpson, according to his biographer Mark Junge, entered the West in 1889. Stimpson's photographs are distinctive. Junge claims "His turn-of-the-century photographs of the Union Pacific, for example, are unique as a visual cross section of the West during a transitional period in its history, a time when it was emerging from frontier status. The consistently well-composed and sharply focused images document a 500 mile long corridor flanking a railroad that lay between the Missouri River and the West Coast." Green River and Rock Springs were two of the towns Stimpson photographed.[56]

Stimpson's 1903 photographs captured the nature of the buildings in both Rock Springs and Green River. Like Jackson and Russell earlier, Stimpson was impressed with the panorama at Green River. Like the others, he photographed the majestic buttes and sharp cliff walls above the Green River. But Stimpson was also interested in what some viewed as commonplace. He photographed the Green River Brewery, tie drives on the Green River, and the railroad bridge across the river. At Rock Springs he photographed the mines and took two panoramic shots that provide us with some of our best glimpses of Rock Springs at the turn of the century. In 1900 there were 4,363 residents of Rock Springs; by 1920 the number had climbed to 6,456. One-third of the residents in 1920 were foreign-born. The census keepers of the era divided people into categories of "Native born," "Foreign born," "Negro" and "Others." In the year 1920, there were 160 Others and 62 Negroes living within the city limits. In 1900 there were 2,059 Native born, 2,304 Foreign born, and 518 Negro residents in Rock Springs.[57]

As the twentieth century dawned, rumors abounded that a soda plant would be built in Green River. A report on the front page of the Cheyenne Daily Sun Leader on January 31, 1899, a "glass manufacturer" was hoping to build a plant in Green River. Soda, or trona, is a basic element in glass manufacturing. In 1899, the possibility of a plant was just that, an unfulfilled hope. It would not be until years later that the city's dreams of tapping its vast soda resources were realized, but nonetheless, the Green River Star called on the city's businesses "to get together and establish a board of trade for the purpose of distributing information to the outside world in regard" to the areas resources.[58] By 1903 the soda plant was a reality.

There were periods between 1900 and 1920 when economic downturns occurred, but overall there was continuous growth in

(Top) Ezra Emery photograph showing freight train hauling wool in the early 1900s, in Rock Springs.

(Bottom) Bridge across Henry's Fork, "taken by Mrs. A. S. Davis at Burnt Fork, July 1, 1900."

(Top) Photograph "taken by Mrs. Agnes S. Davis at Burnt Fork, July 3rd 1900."

(Bottom) Blacksmith shops were the "mechanic's garage" before the car was invented. Many blacksmiths made the transition to auto repairmen. Courtesy of the Wyoming State Archives, Museums and Historical Department, Cheyenne.

both the Green River and Rock Springs areas during this time period. The Rock Springs that Stimpson photographed in 1903 was a coal town that consisted of diverse groups of people. In 1920, little had changed. There were Greeks, Italians, Slovenians, Serbians, Austrians, Carniolans, Japanese, Dalmatians, Croatians, English, Finlanders, Germans, Hungarians, Irish, Poles, Russians, Scots, Romanians, Swedes, Tyroleans, and Welsh all living in Rock Springs. The emigrants came seeking opportunity. Many found difficulties and prejudices. Yet, in the end, they welded together the community of Rock Springs.[59]

After the turn of the century, the nature of mining began to change in the Rock Springs area. Shortly before the 1900 and in the early 1900s, coal camps opened outside Rock Springs. A. R. Schultz, in his 1908 report for the U.S. Geological Survey, sums up this change when he writes: "From the completion of the Union Pacific in 1869 to the construction of the Superior branch up Horse Thief Canyon in 1906, all the mining camps in the Rock Springs field, except the Sweetwater camp south of Rock Springs, were opened along the railroad in Bitter Creek Valley at distances of less than a mile from the main line."[60] As Schultz notes, early mining occurred directly adjacent to the Union Pacific main line. After 1906 when the Superior railspur was completed, other towns began appearing north of the rail line. For instance, towns like East Plane, Lionkol, Winton, and later, Stansbury sprang up north of Rock Springs. Most of these coal towns emerged between 1910 and 1940. The towns of Superior, Gunn, Winton, Reliance, and Dines all came into existence between 1903 and 1920.

At the turn of the century, there were four coal mining districts in Sweetwater County. These districts consisted of Rock Springs, Superior, Point of Rocks, and Black Butte.[61] The Rock Springs district was the oldest and largest. It was defined as "all the coal-bearing beds north and south of Bitter Creek Valley on the west side of the dome in the vicinity of Rock Springs, or that part of Little Bitter Creek and Killpecker Valleys whose source of supply and transportation centers around Rock Springs."[62] Within this district,

Rock Springs No. 9 coal mine around the turn of the century. Courtesy of the Wyoming State Archives, Museums and Historical Department, Cheyenne.

there were seven mining camps in 1908. These camps included Rock Springs, Sweetwater (later called Quealy), Blairtown, No. 6, Interstate, Van Dyk, and Gunn. The Point of Rocks District encompassed the area surrounding Point of Rocks. In 1908 only one mine was operating in the district.[63] The Black Butte District consisted of all coal-bearing beds from the Point of Rocks District southward to Black Butte Creek. When Schultz conducted his survey, only the Gibraltar Mine was actually operating in the Black Buttes District. The other district was the then newly-opened Superior District, which was confined to the northern end of Horse Thief Canyon. In 1907 at Superior, five mines including A Mine, B Mine, C Mine, D Mine, and E Mine were in operation.[64]

The years leading up to World War I witnessed an increased amount of coal production from Sweetwater County. With the rising demand for coal, new jobs were created and people moved into the area seeking employment. In ten years the number of people living in the county increased by 61 percent. Specifically, the population of Sweetwater County grew from 8,455 in 1910 to 13,640 in 1920, with most of this growth occurring in the new coal towns such as Superior and South Superior. There were no residents of these two towns in 1905, but by 1920 their combined population had reached 1,453.[65] The majority of the people moving to these new towns were coal miners. The Wyoming Census for 1915 showed that 38 percent of all the miners working in the state of Wyoming lived in Sweetwater County.[66]

At the turn of the century, Sweetwater County residents lived primarily in villages or towns. These towns came into existence to serve the coal mines and the railroad. The people of Sweetwater County were primarily town dwellers.

Sweetwater County courthouse in Green River, 1903. Courtesy of the Wyoming State Archives, Museums and Historical Department, Cheyenne, J. E. Stimpson Collection.

Morris Mercantile Company store, Green River, Wyoming, 1903. Courtesy of the Wyoming State Archives, Museums and Historical Department, Cheyenne, J. E. Stimpson Collection.

Tea Kettle Rock, Green River Wyoming, 1903. Courtesy of the Wyoming State Archives, Museums and Historical Department, Cheyenne, J. E. Stimpson Collection.

Union Pacific Bridge and Castle Rock, 1903. Courtesy of the Wyoming State Archives, Museums and Historical Department, Cheyenne, J. E. Stimpson Collection.

Green River, 1902-1903; this building sat at the corner of Railroad and First.

Hazel Hay Gibson on the Bridge over Bitter Creek in Rock Springs in 1905.

Chinese New Year parade on North Front Street, Rock Springs, in 1906.

"Harney and Stowe Freighters" at Green River
preparing to haul the "Brewery's Beer Wagon."

Looking east toward Toll Gate west of Green
River (photograph undated).

"Japanese Town" at Superior about 1907 or 1908. This community was separated from the main coal camp. It, along with Chinatown in Rock Springs, reflects a conscious policy to segregate Asians from other miners.

"Garr Scott Tractor" pulling eight plows in order to demonstrate its power. Walt and Earl Wright are riding on the machine—"400 acres of land in the spring of 1911 were plowed with this tractor."

This was probably the mine foreman's home at Gibraltar. The chisel marks of stonemasons are visible in the cornerstones. Using locally available stone, these masons crafted a small mansion to house the foreman at the mine. The Gibralter coal mine dates to the first decade of the 1900s.

The Gibraltar mine experienced its heyday at the turn of the century. Remains of the mine exhibit the craftsmanship of the stone masons.

Freight wagons headed for Pinedale in 1908. The trip from Rock Springs to Pinedale took five days. Photograph taken facing the corner of K Street and Pilot Butte in Rock Springs.

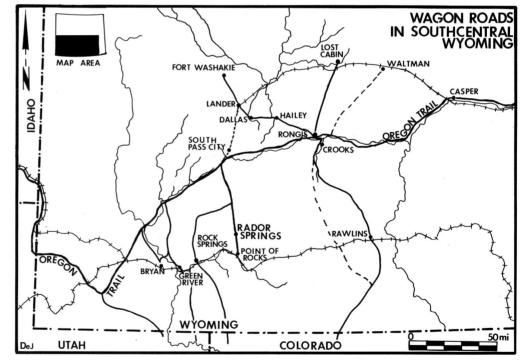

With the completion of the railroad in 1868, transportation networks were established from the railroad to towns north and south of the Union Pacific main line. Stock trails, stage lines, and freight roads all led to the railroad.

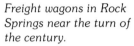

Freight wagons in Rock Springs near the turn of the century.

Wagon owned by Bunning Transfer Company in Rock Springs. Freighting by wagons was the most common form of shipping locally at the turn of the century.

Goods being freighted from Rock Springs by "Mr. Charles Shedden."

The steamboat Comet *on the Green River in Sweetwater County in July of 1908.*

Green River Navigation Company, Inc. in 1908 owned the Comet. It was used for carrying freight from Green River to Henry's Fork.

The earliest written records of floating the Green River began with William Ashley in 1825. However, John Wesley Powell's famous expedition down the Green in 1869 is the best known. Powell started his trip on or near Expedition Island.

(Top) The steamboat Comet in 1908. The Comet ran up and down the Green River carrying passengers and freight."

(Bottom) R. H. Watt at the Palisades near Green River Wyoming, 1907–1910.

(Top) Immersion baptism at Farson, on the Sandy River, 1910 or 1922. Shown here are Reverend Rambo and Lovilla Henderson; Helen Rambo, Reverend Rambo's daughter, is awaiting her turn.

(Bottom) "A picnic at Eagle Rock six miles east of Farson on Highway 28." Left to right: Elizabeth Wright, Allie Sims, Gertie Sims, Pearl Goodrich, and Bill Sims.

Picnic at Eagle Rock near Farson (photograph not dated).

Photograph of United States Geological Survey (USGS) crew crossing the Killpecker Dune Fields circa 1907. Courtesy of the USGS Photographic Library, Denver.

The Lincoln Highway west of Green River in the early 1900s.

Approximate route of the Lincoln Highway, one of the first interstate automobile routes across the nation. In 1908 the "Great Auto Race" around the world used the Lincoln Highway as a portion of its route.

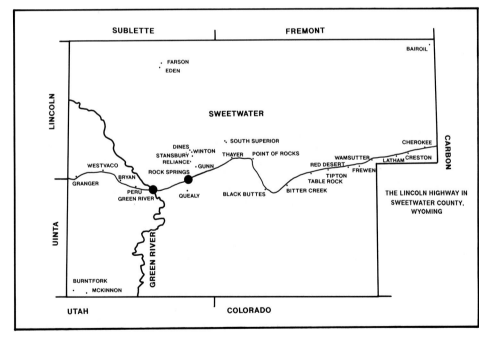

SUBLETTE FREMONT

BAIROIL

LINCOLN

· FARSON
· EDEN

SWEETWATER

CARBON

· SOUTH SUPERIOR

CHEROKEE

DINES
STANSBURY · WINTON
RELIANCE THAYER POINT OF ROCKS
WESTVACO · GUNN WAMSUTTER LATHAM CRESTON
BRYAN ROCK SPRINGS RED DESERT FREWEN
GRANGER TIPTON
PERU QUEALY TABLE ROCK
GREEN RIVER BLACK BUTTES BITTER CREEK

THE LINCOLN HIGHWAY IN
SWEETWATER COUNTY,
WYOMING

UINTA

GREEN RIVER

BURNTFORK
· MCKINNON

UTAH COLORADO

(Top) USGS survey crew south of Rock Springs conducting its survey in 1907. They tipped their wagon and lost part of their load in this unnamed arroyo. (Courtesy USGS Photographic Library, Denver)

USGS survey crew's camp near Black Butte, circa 1906-1907. Note the water wagon and stack of wood. Provision of water and fuel was essential in undeveloped country. Courtesy of the USGS Photographic Library, Denver.

This photograph dates to 1906 or 1907 and shows the Point of Rocks to South Pass stage road. Also shown is A. R. Schultz' survey team. Courtesy of the USGS Photographic Library, Denver.

Richard's Gap Stage Station circa 1906 or 1907, taken by A. R. Schultz of the USGS survey team. This stage station was located on the Rock Springs to Vernal stageline, just north of the Utah border in Sweetwater County. Courtesy of the USGS Photographic Library, Denver.

"Custom harvesters," probably in the Eden Valley (photograph not dated).

The "Great Auto Race" of 1908 passed through Rock Springs and Green River in that year. French, Italian, German, and American teams raced west during the winter. Eventually the French team dropped out and the Americans won.

Photograph of the 1908 "Great Race." This event was later portrayed in a movie staring Jack Lemmon and Natalie Wood. Enthusiastic onlookers greeted the racers as they ran through downtown Rock Springs and Green River.

A crew of railroad tie-drivers on a brief respite during the process of floating the ties south. Pictured on a gravel bar in the Green River (photograph not dated).

Parade in Rock Springs, around the turn of the century.

Chapter III
THE WEALTH BENEATH OUR FEET

f you climb to the top of Pilot Butte and look to the east and west, you can view nearly a hundred miles of what appears to be empty expanses. In reality, the areas east and west contain miles and miles of tunnels beneath the earth. To the east, historic coal mines and present-day mining operations have undercut the surface. To the west, some of the largest underground mines ever excavated extract trona. Even deeper than the coal and trona lies natural gas—Wyoming boasts world-class natural gas deposits. Combined, these natural resources make Sweetwater County one of the wealthiest counties in the state.[1]

When Wyoming became a state in 1890, its economy centered around agriculture, mining, the service industries, transportation, and tourism. In 1993, the county's economy still depends on these for its economic well-being. For Sweetwater County, transportation and mining are the basis of the economy. Mining involves removing resources from beneath the ground. The extraction of petroleum, natural gas, and even helium or any other gas is all part of a mining process. The key to defining mining is the extraction or removal of resources from beneath the surface. In Sweetwater County the economy has always depended primarily on the extractive industries for its prosperity. Transportation, both by rail and by semi-tractors and trailers, is also a major source of revenue. The service industries, although often overlooked, are a key component in the economy. While agriculture has never generated as much revenue as mining or the railroad, it has been an important part of the region since 1843. Cattle and sheep are evident throughout most of the county. In viewing the landscape one can readily see how ranching still dominates the region's agricultural industry. Continuity prevails. From 1868 to today, the source of wealth has changed little.

Around the turn of the century, Sweetwater County's economy

To grow a garden in Rock Springs, or any other place in Sweetwater County, took patience and effort. This is the Antonia Frank house in July 1922. On the left is Mrs. Rose Morgan. Frank Morgan stands in the garden. Franc Burnik, on the swing, is the father of Annie Burnik Tucker. Courtesy of the New Studio, Rock Springs.

(Top) The Union Pacific Coal Company store or Superior Coal Company (SCC) store built in 1908. SCC was actually a wholly-owned subsidiary of Union Pacific and Company.

(Bottom) Finnish miners at the Black Buttes Railroad station. These miners worked and owned their own coal mine (photograph undated).

looked much like it did in 1868. Coal mining employed the majority of the men. The Union Pacific railroad stationed repair crews on the mainline from Wamsutter to Church Buttes, and also on the Oregon Short Line running north from Granger into future Lincoln County. Like railroad section crews in the 1870s, crews in the early 1900s who were employed to repair the right-of-way lived in section camps scattered throughout the county. Ranchers herded cattle through the sage, and homesteaders could be found scattered in isolated pockets throughout the county. Yet, for all the continuity, there were winds of change. Two industries were waiting in the wings, destined to emerge as eventual giants in the local economy. The first was the petroleum industry; the second was the production of soda ash.

The presence of oil in Wyoming was known by Indians, trappers, and overland emigrants. Emigrants bound westward over South Pass had used crude oil found in pools along the Oregon Trail to grease the axles of their wagons. It was well known by the turn of the century that oil abounded in Sweetwater County. The potential for large scale development was obvious.

The impetus that gave rise to a booming Wyoming oil industry was the development of the automobile. "In 1900, only 8,000 passenger automobiles had been registered in the United States; by 1905, the number of registrations had increased tenfold to 77,000."[2] In 1906, 106,000 passenger cars traveled America's highways. The year 1908 witnessed the "Great New York to Paris Automobile Race" through Rock Springs and Green River and it was in this year that Henry Ford introduced the fabled Model T. It was a revolutionary event. The price of a car was under fifteen hundred dollars and many Americans could now afford the new gas-burning horseless carriages.[3] So popular was the car that by 1919 the number of registered passenger vehicles was 6,771,000; ten years later this number stood at 23,122,000.[4] Gasoline was needed to fuel these new cars and the state of Wyoming was rich in petroleum.

Early references to oil development in Sweetwater County are scattered and sketchy. By 1920, it was known that places like Baxter Basin, Baroil, Powder Wash, and Hiawatha contained crude oil. It was also known that natural gas abounded. In the future, natural gas would prove to be more abundant than petroleum. But at the turn of the century, oil men wanted "black gold."

Ezra Emery, manager of Union Pacific Coal Company's waterworks, reported that a "Belgo" company was drilling wells in Sweetwater County in 1909. While Emery does not describe Belgo's operation, it appears this oil company was soliciting funds by selling stock to local investors. It was not a successful venture and in a letter to a friend, Mrs. D. M. Thayer, he warned: "I got your Belgo American circular—looks worse than that here. Don't quote me . . . but I'll just give you a quiet tip." The sheriff, Ezra wrote, "is out to the wells in this county today trying to find something upon which to put a mechanics lien. Belgo people have not dug up anything but promises for six months."[5] Other early twentieth-century ventures proved potentially more profitable. Investment in oil development at the turn of the century, however, was often speculative at best.

As early as 1895, an edition of the *Cheyenne Daily Leader* anticipated both the oil boom and the development of Wyoming's soda ash deposits. The paper was attempting to attract investors to Wyoming. The *Leader* proclaimed: "There are great opportunities for the profitable employment of capital in the oil fields of the state. . . . Once the ball is set to rolling this great natural resource will add thousands upon thousands to the population of Wyoming and millions and millions of dollars to its taxable wealth."[6] At the time, most of the marketable soda ash came from playa lakes in Carbon County, Wyoming. Yet, the paper noted: "soda offers tempting inducements" for developers and also for "the manufacturers of glass and soap."[7] The *Daily Leader* was anticipating, rather than reporting on large scale development of these two industries. Large scale development of Wyoming oil and soda would not occur until the twentieth century. Nonetheless, the *Daily Leader* proved prophetic in anticipating the growth of these two industries.

Ranching in the early part of the twentieth century underwent a boom. This was due, in part, to more generous homesteading laws that allowed ranchers to claim more land than when

The wooden coal tipple at Reliance, circa 1910-1920. This wooden tipple was replaced with a steel tipple in 1936.

homesteading began. Also, a nationwide "back-to-the-country move-ment" drew women homesteaders such as Elinore Pruitt Stuart to southwestern Wyoming.

The Enlarged Homestead Act of 1909 led to a rush to western lands. The Act was designed to encourage dryland farming on non-irrigatable, non-mineral lands that had no merchantable timber within the states of Colorado, Montana, Nevada, Oregon, Utah, Washing-ton, Wyoming, and the territories of Arizona and New Mexico. The Act allowed the homesteader to obtain 320 acres of land. Interest-ingly, this Homestead Act actually reflects Theodore Roosevelt's concept of conservation. Roosevelt wrote: "Conservation is not keeping [land] out of use, but is putting things to the best use without waste, and where possible, preserving their potential useful-ness unimpaired."[8]

Roosevelt sought a land policy that would aid the individual landowner. During his presidential campaign of 1912, Roosevelt proclaimed: "All the nation's natural resources should be handled and administered in the interest of 'the actual settler, the actual homemaker.'"[9] Although Roosevelt was not re-elected in 1912, the ground he broke bore fruit in 1916. The Stock Raising Homestead Act became law and increased the amount of land a person could claim from 320 acres to 640 acres. The net result of these changes was an increased amount of homesteading activity in places like Sweetwater County.

In the first two decades of the twentieth century, there was a "back-to-the-country movement." It is not possible to date when this phenomenon began, but the March 12, 1910, issue of *Colliers Magazine* stated: "back to the country is a topic more than ever before discussed and dreamed about by city people."[10] Numerous city dwellers felt the pressures of their urban surroundings. "The rising expenses and accelerating pace of city life [prompted] large numbers of city dwellers to seek" what was perceived as "a simpler and saner environment." Colliers pointed out in 1910 that there was already a tide "of migration toward the village and the farm."[11] The back-to-the-land movement was discussed in numerous publications of the period and numerous people were convinced to give up their life in the city for a better life in the country.

When Elinore Pruitt Stewart moved to the Henry's Fork Valley in Sweetwater County to live on a homestead, she was acting out the sentiments of an age. When she wrote her letters, she was writing to an audience that wanted to hear what she had to say about life in the rural West, or more importantly, what life was like in the

This Sweetwater County farmer, John Wright, is showing off the oats he grew in 1912.

country. On January 23, 1913 she wrote from her home in Sweetwater County, "To me, homesteading is the solution of all poverty's problems." Yet she knew homesteading was not for everyone. She wrote: "I realize that temperament has much to do with success in any undertaking, and persons afraid of coyotes and work and loneliness had better let ranching alone. At the same time, any woman who can stand her own company, can see the beauty of the sunset, loves growing things, and is willing to put in as much time at careful labor as she does over the washtub, will certainly succeed; will have independence, plenty to eat all the time, and a home of her own in the end."[12] Mrs. Stewart was reflecting a widely-held attitude. She wrote her popular work in her Wyoming home.

In nearly every American history textbook the reader is told "that with the Gilded Age, rural Americans started moving to the cities in significant numbers."[13] This trend of moving into cities accelerated "to the point that by 1920 the population of the United was predominantly urban." In their haste to simplify the historic process and present students with generalities about American history, authors often fail to mention that "this demographic shift did not proceed on a one-way street."[14] In fact, "there was a heavy flow of population in both directions, from country to the city, and from the city to the country" throughout the first three decades of the twentieth century.[15] More people did move to the cities, "but beginning in the first decade of the century, and rolling into the second under a full head of steam, was a collective passion, indeed, an emotional contagion, among urban Americans: to gain ownership of their own tract of farmland."[16] "This," according to historian Stanford Layton, "was the back-to-the-land movement and a very sizeable movement it was."

Barbara Allen, in her work *Homesteading the High Desert,* explains several motives behind homesteading efforts in the early twentieth century. She states. "The Back-to-the-Land promoters were true progressives in their desire to save the city by redeeming

(Top) These tracks were laid to allow the transport of coal from the mine to the tipple at Reliance. Over a mile of trackage was laid between the mine and the tipple. Photograph dated September 22, 1913.

(Bottom) North Front Street and the Vienna Cafe, Rock Springs, in 1915. Courtesy of the New Studio, Rock Springs.

the countryside through the efficient use of resources."[17] Quoting from William L. O'Neill, Allen contends: "Given the long-standing American view 'that farmers were naturally virtuous and freedom loving pillars of democracy unlike the decadent aristocrats, wretched aliens, and greedy businessmen of Urban America' to save American people most move back to the country."[18] Dr. Allen goes on to state: ". . . the growth of an urbanized citizenry raised the specter of a nation bereft of its traditional conservative values." Thus, going back to the land might create new values or re-enforce old traditional values. "One response to this potential threat was the Back-to-the-Land movement, aimed at creating a best-of-both-worlds synthesis of the city and the country." Some homesteaders came to Sweetwater County to pursue the myth of finding a simple, more virtuous lifestyle. Allen states: "The chief promoters of the Back-to-the-Land movement—politicians, lawyers, educators, speculators, bankers, and the like—proceeded from the assumption that the cities were over-populated while the rural districts were correspondingly under-populated."[19] Elinore Pruitt Stewart, who wrote her letters in Sweetwater County, was writing to an audience wanting to hear about the virtues of homesteading. From Burnt Fork she reached a national audience.

(Top) Old Union Hall Saloon and Chicago Meat Market in 1915. In Rock Springs commerce centered around serving coal miners and their families. Courtesy of the New Studio, Rock Springs.

(Bottom) Train wreck near Rock Springs "taken before 1915."

Homesteading increased countywide, but possibly one of the most heavily homesteaded areas was in the Eden Valley. The history of agriculture in the Eden Valley is older than is apparent at first glance. Possibly the first ranchers in the area herded cattle for the stage stations along the Oregon Trail, or perhaps some of the herders listed in the 1860 census ran their cattle in the valley. Nonetheless, by the 1890s, homesteaders were beginning to settle into making the area a permanent ranching community. Mrs. Elizabeth Apperson, along with her husband William Apperson, settled on the Little Sandy in 1891.[20] The Apperson family "was among the early pioneers who crossed the plains with teams on the old Oregon Trail in the early days." Interestingly, it was claimed these homesteaders "crossed the plains in prairie schooners five times from Missouri, their native state. They were on their sixth trip from Washington when they wintered at Lander [during] the winter of '90 and '91."[21] It was during this winter that they decided to return to Sweetwater County and settle on the Little Sandy. "In the spring of '91, they came with Jack Piper, a settler of the Eden country at that time, to Eden where they lived on the Little Sandy." They moved, in 1894, to the Green River Valley and located a home on Horse Creek. While they lived in the Eden Valley, "they also supplied many residents in Rock Springs with elk meat." According to one report, in the 1890s, elk were "plentiful on the plains north" of Rock Springs.[22]

Permits for irrigating within the Eden Valley were first filed around the turn of the century. In 1905, the Eden Irrigation and Land Company was incorporated and in the following year "56,322.74 acres of public land withdrawn."[23] Eden Valley histo-

Butcher shop in Green River, circa 1915–1916.

rian, Linda Simnacher, writes: "The potential of the Eden project was given added credibility when the University of Wyoming established an experiment farm at Eden in 1907."[24] Water for large-scale irrigation was first delivered to Farson in 1908 and to Eden the next year. Hampered by the environment and the lack of a reservoir on the Big Sandy, area residents valiantly labored to make a go of their homesteads in the Valley. It would not be until 1952 that the long-proposed and hoped for reservoir on the Big Sandy would be completed.[25]

South of Rock Springs along Currant and Sage Creeks, homesteaders built houses and plowed the valleys. They constructed irrigation ditches, built corrals, and raised families. Rose Teters Logan, whose family lived on Sage Creek recalls: "we had quite a few sheep one time, but they got so they were too much bother for us to have to watch." It was difficult to run the ranch and Rose states all work

In 1918, the highway west from Green River was little more than a two-track road. Automobile travel at the time was fraught with obstacles, including getting stuck or stranded in isolated areas.

was done by "horse power, mowing machine, rakes, bull rakes, but everything was horsepower. Never did have machinery." We grew "alfalfa, hay, grain, grew our own vegetables, potatoes, carrots [and] beets."[26] Rose milked the cows and they had fresh milk.[27] In reality, homesteading was hard work. The romance of the back-to-country movement rarely entered into the minds of people milking cows or pulling weeds.

Within the towns of Sweetwater County, emigrants worked and labored to make ends meet. Slovenian women made sausages and helped butcher chickens. Italian women, to help support their families, took in men boarders who worked in the coal mines. Many women in Superior and other coal towns in the county did laundry for single coal miners to bring in additional revenues. During World War I, the women worked as laborers on the railroad. Whether they lived on a homestead or lived in a coal town, women contributed much to the economy.

World War I had a profound effect on Sweetwater County. Rock Springs and Superior were towns made up of emigrants from Asia and Europe. The Europeans included English, Germans, and Slovenians. In Europe, their relatives were engulfed in a life-and-death struggle. In the United States, they were torn by the desire to

Funeral for T. J. Walen, April 4, 1921. Walen served in World War I. Courtesy of the New Studio, Rock Springs.

serve their adopted country but at the same time they experienced an abiding concern for loved ones left in Europe. There were tensions.

The news of the outbreak of war was greeted with patriotic fervor in Green River and Rock Springs. The *Rock Springs Miner* in April of 1917 noted that their town set out to do its patriotic duty. The recruiting officer was one E. F. Stodmaster, "chief gunners mate." The B.P.O. Elks of Rock Springs, together with the postmaster, took the lead in obtaining recruits, holding nightly mass meetings where "everybody wears a flag and patriotism is at a high pitch." Every night these citizens placed "a brass drum on the streets and the citizens threw coins upon the drum, the contributions going to the young men who enlist." The "gunners mate" noted that "the Elks gave $10 to each recruit."[28] Rock Springs and Green River sent large numbers of their young men to fight in what President Woodrow Wilson proclaimed was the "war to end all wars."

Women in Sweetwater County worked at a variety of jobs during World War I. Union Pacific Railroad announced in December of 1917: "in order that their male ticket agents may be relieved from usual duties and replace men who went to the armies" beginning immediately, they would "place women ticket agents at all important ticket offices of that road throughout the country."[29] Before the war was over, women worked on maintenance-of-the-way crews. Based on photographs that survive from the period, it appears some crews were entirely female.

In many ways, the foreign-born residents of the county tried hard to prove they were patriotic. "Were every county as patriotic as Sweetwater," the Rock Springs newspaper proclaimed, "there would be no need of those posters calling on our young men to join the army or navy." On September 18, sixty boys from Sweetwater

(Top) Evers Brothers' "Green River Lumber Shop" located on Blake Street.

(Bottom) This undated photograph shows the Green River Band in front of the "Old Court House."

(Top) Green River Wyoming, Lumber Company In front are Edith and E. E. Peters, the proprietors (photograph not dated).

(Bottom) The "Second Masonic Hall" in Green River. Note the wheels of what may be a Model T on the left side of the photograph.

County left Green River for the training ground.[30] Hundreds ultimately left the county to serve in the army, the aviation corps, and the navy. On September 28, 1917, it was reported that since April 1, 1917, 233 volunteers were recruited in Rock Springs alone.[31] Foreign-born nationals were among the recruits.

At Slovenski Dom in Rock Springs, the "Slovac People," held a patriotic meeting on September 30, 1917. Slovenski Dom is the building where the Slovenians held their gatherings. On that day, the Rock Springs "Branch No. 113, Slovak League of America" issued the following proclamation: "Be It Therefore Resolved, that we, American citizens, residents of Rock Springs Wyoming on the 30th day of September, in mass meeting assembled, express our unflinching determination to do all that is within our power, together with the American government and America Allies in this great struggle in order that our kins, the Slovaks, the Bohemians, the Poles, and the Southern Slavs across the sea, may forever be liberated and set free."[32] The resolution went on to proclaim, hereby pledge ourselves to adopt the stars and stripes as our flag and never under any circumstances will serve another."[33]

As fatalities grew and reports of Sweetwater County men dying in France arrived, tensions mounted. By February 18, 1918, Sweetwater County had sent 440 men to the front in France.[34] Coupled with the first fatalities, the fact such a large portion of the young male population was overseas led to ethnic conflict. In Superior, a "100 Per Cent American Club" was organized.[35] Reliance organized a fledgling "club" at the same time. In Cheyenne, "The 100 Percent American Society" on February 1, 1918, announced they would "use yellow paint on residents of their section who show Pro-German tendencies, even though they do not entirely overstep what would be termed a legal disloyalty charge."[36] The Cheyenne "Society" said this move "should be adopted in every community in Wyoming." And the editor of the Miner wrote, "it might be especially useful in Rock Springs where a number of such persons are to be found. . . ."[37] It was not long before words became actions. Rock Springs was little different than some other cities in its response. What was different was that this coal camp, and places such as Superior and Reliance as well, had large numbers of "Foreign born aliens." Early in February "21 German Alien Enemies Registered" in Rock Springs.[38] On April 12, 1918, "two disloyal Austrians were jailed."[39] At Winton, a German sympathizer was arrested and brought into Rock Springs until "Federal authorities could make an investigation."[40] Yet, in light of the large numbers of Germans, Austrians, and others born in countries supporting the Axis nations, there was less violence than might have erupted in such a heterogenous community. In part, this was due to many foreign-born aliens wanting to prove their patriotism.

Throughout Sweetwater County an outpouring of patriotism emerged. The chair of the Women's Liberty Loan Committee, Mrs. T. S. Taliaferro, reported that residents of Wamsutter were buying bonds and doing "everything and anything that could help in winning the war and help to make the boys comfortable who are fighting in the war." As the result of Taliaferro's visit to Wamsutter, it was reported that while "the community is not large in number of souls . . . it is large in enthusiasm and broad in ways of thinking and full of energy to do something."[41] Labor Day 1918 was called Liberty Day in Rock Springs and reportedly the "largest parade ever witnessed" in local history was to be held.

Sweetwater County purchased hundreds of thousands of dollars worth of Liberty Bonds. The North Side State Bank sold $63,100; the First National of Rock Springs, $118,750; and people in the town of Green River purchased $59,000. Superior, the third largest town in the county, sold $76,950. In all, by mid-April, the county had subscribed to $600,000 worth of war bonds.[42] Considering salaries in 1918, the amount purchased was impressive. When the

Holmes Ferry on the Green River. Shown here are Maria "Mayme" Kidd, Frank Kidd, and Robby Gillum.

Junior High School band in the 1920s.

war ended on November 11, 1918, Sweetwater County had done more than its share. It provided coal for trains and ships, men for the front, and money to pursue the war.

The end of World War I and the beginning of a new decade was met with great expectations in Sweetwater County. Yet several facts worked to dim the potential economic growth that many expected. The first was Prohibition. In Sweetwater County, Prohibition had a checkered history, but essentially the people in the county worked hard to insure that while the law said the nation was to be dry, the desert did not have to be. The second factor was more critical. Prices for coal and agricultural goods were depressed in the years shortly after World War I. Especially hard-hit were the West's coal mining regions. In the 1920s the conversion from coal to oil as the principal form of fossil fuel began to take hold. Some communities in Wyoming benefited from this change, and interest increased in developing the natural gas and petroleum deposits in Sweetwater County. In many ways, it was the beginning of an economic transition. Ultimately the petroleum industry, coupled with the commercial development of natural gas fields in the county, would emerge as an important part of the economy, but for the time being, "King coal" was suffering an economic reversal and the county was feeling the effect.[43]

Prohibition created one of the more colorful periods in the history of the county. To emigrants who had always made wine, even in Sweetwater County where grapes had to be shipped in, the attempt to end the consumption of alcoholic beverages seemed to make little sense. Wine was considered a part of meals. To stop producing wine seemed unthinkable. Moreover, now anyone who made wine at home became a potential moonshiner and might make extra revenue during a time when Sweetwater County's economy was in transition.

To emigrant children fell the job of stomping grapes to make wine. Rock Springs' residents, Eugene Paoli and Antone Pivik, retain clear memories of how wine and moonshine were made. Eugene Paoli states: "I stomped many grapes. Dad would get those fishing boots and wash them off. . . . By the time you got through with two tons of grapes, boy, that's a lot of stomping."[44] Antone Pivik relates they would then make wine, "they would ferment it right off the first batch. The second batch they would add a little sugar to it and would ferment it again and make second wine. But then you take all the rest of the stuff that is left and add more sugar. Then we would distill that and make graupa."[45] Graupa was pure moonshine. And according to Eugene Paoli, "when you went down to No. 4 Town" on the east side of Rock Springs, "you could really smell the moonshine." Especially when they threw "out the old mash after all the whiskey was out of it. They would try and bury it in the garden, but you couldn't miss" the smell.[46]

Running moonshine involved a number of different tactics, and numerous stories emerge about how Rock Springs residents outwitted local "revenuers." It has become a touchstone in the 1920s to tell about moonshiners or one's involvement in the process of making or consuming "white lightening." One story that has come down in a variety of forms deals with a moonshiner and his son who made a delivery of "Rock Springs Moon" to Salt Lake City. While driving down State Street, in Salt Lake City, a tire on their car went flat. In the trunk they had their moonshine. Apparently, the spare tire was mounted outside the trunk on a tire rack. The

(Top) Alfred Richmond won third prize for this garden at Reliance, circa 1920s.

(Bottom) George Snyder won first prize from the Union Pacific Coal Company for this garden he planted in Reliance. The coal company, in an attempt to improve the image of their coal towns, gave yearly prizes for the best garden in the "desert."

details of the story are clouded by time and the retelling of the tale.

Broken down on State Street, the moonshiner and his son attracted the attention of a Salt Lake City policeman, who offered to help change the tire. The son could speak English, the father could not. The son thanked the officer and together they changed the tire. When they were finished, the father told the son to give the kind man a bottle of moonshine. A fight followed with the son arguing loudly and pleadingly that this was Salt Lake City and not Rock Springs. They could be arrested for transporting moonshine. The officer could not understand the argument and ultimately they went their separate ways, no one the wiser for the misunderstanding. True or false, the story reflects a glimpse into the folklore surrounding Prohibition. Moreover, the father may well have thought it proper etiquette to give a policeman moonshine, if that is what he did in Rock Springs when one assisted him.

The repeal of the Eighteenth Amendment meant alcohol could once again be legally sold in Sweetwater County. The era of Prohibition had ended. Lasting from 1919 to 1933, Prohibition was greeted with similar reactions in the coal camps throughout southwestern Wyoming. The Eighteenth Amendment simply had driven wine and whiskey making underground.

In the 1920s Sweetwater County underwent a transition that is not readily apparent at first glance. For years the county had depended on the railroad and coal for its economic foundation. Service industries, such as banking and retailing along with ranching and, to a lesser degree, tourism, provided some revenues but the bedrock of the economy had been mining and transportation. This was about to change. As the use of machinery grew, the need for coal miners decreased. More importantly, petroleum was becoming more widely used as a source of fossil fuel than coal. Natural gas slowly became an alternative to coal for heating homes.

As coal contracts vanished, so did towns in Sweetwater County that depended on coal for their existence. By the end of the 1930s, Gibraltar and Gunn either no longer existed or were shadows of their former selves. The loss of revenues

(Top) Downtown Rock Springs, showing both the historic city hall and post office. Probably this photograph dates to the late 1910s or early 1920s.

(Bottom) Street Dance in Rock Springs in the 1920s.

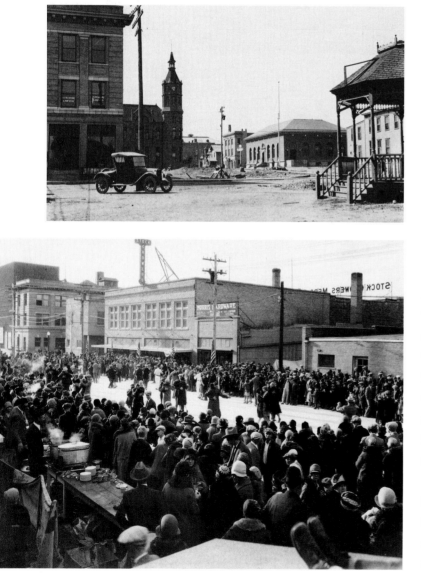

due to the decreasing demand for coal affected Rock Springs and Superior, whose livelihood depended on the mines to fuel their economies. From 1920 to 1932 coal towns waxes and waned, but in the background the oil industry and later natural gas development began to emerge to shore up the local economy. But in the 1920s, at least in Sweetwater County, this industry was in its infancy. People were being drawn to the oil fields in increasing numbers, in fact, statewide the petroleum industry became one of the leading employers; but this was not yet the case in Sweetwater County. In the 1920s, the oil fields of the county were of secondary concern in comparison to places like the Salt Wells field in Natrona County.

Toward the end of the 1920s, changes also appeared on the horizon for the ranching industry. A primary concern to most stockmen and homesteaders in the 1920s was the overgrazed range. Overgrazing had reached the point that Congressman Edward Taylor from Colorado said that there was not a blade of grass left to graze in Wyoming.[47] It was an exaggeration, but it reflects a serious

(Top) Circa 1920s photograph of "S. Ono" car near Rock Springs. Courtesy of the New Studio, Rock Springs.

(Bottom) Funeral for S. Yamasaki, February 1, 1920. Note the Rock Springs Miner's Hospital in the background. Courtesy of the New Studio, Rock Springs.

Oil drilling rig ready to leave Rock Springs during the 1920s. Note the tractor's banner reads: "Lost Creek Consolidated Oil and Gas." Courtesy of the New Studio, Rock Springs.

problem. In addition, agricultural prices were depressed in the years following World War I. While homesteaders worked to improve their land, they often found the price for their products could not cover the cost of those improvements. The ranching industry, of which the small ranchers in Sweetwater County had never been a real part, increasingly required greater amounts of land for a profitable operation. The Taylor Grazing Act of 1934 based the amount of public land that could be leased on the amount of land the rancher owned outright. The Act reflected fact. More land was needed to graze cattle than small homesteaders could hope to control. The days of the small rancher were numbered, and that was becoming apparent in the 1920s.

The stockmarket crash in 1929 did not go unnoticed in Sweetwater County. Yet in many ways, a recession had existed since the early part of the decade. The coal mines still operated but often were idle during the summer months. Homesteaders who settled in Sweetwater County during the first two decades of the twentieth century found prices for their crops were not equal to what had they received during World War I. The expansion of the oil industry in the county was a bright spot in the area's economy, but it did not offset the overall financial outlook to the extent that it would in the future. In fact, by the time of the market crash, Sweetwater County's economy had stabilized. The national depression simply compounded existing problems and did not lead to any immediate changes in the local economy.

In November of 1930 the Wyoming State Federation of Labor and the United Mine Workers of America (UMWA) united their efforts to urge Wyoming citizens to burn coal as a means of reducing unemployment. They also opposed the rising use of natural gas in homes. The UMWA claimed that one way they could lessen the problem and stem the growing "unemployment among the coal miners" was to encourage homeowners to use coal.[48] Rock Springs, Superior and other southwestern Wyoming coal camps stood to benefit from the use of coal-fired home heaters. Yet many felt there was no real unemployment problem in Rock Springs. Union Pacific Coal Company official, George B. Pryde, "stated that there was no alarming unemployment situation in Rock Springs."[49]

The unemployment problem might not have been alarming to Mr.

Pryde; he had a job. Pryde later admitted that while "the coal mine payroll of the Union Pacific Coal company is normal . . . the railway payroll has fallen off slightly."[50] The old adage seemed to apply: "a recession is when you're working and can't pay the bills, a depression is when you don't have a job." In spite of Pryde's rosy outlook in this speech delivered to the Rock Springs Lions Club, that same organization appointed a committee "to investigate the condition of employment with the view of helping the situation if need be."[51]

Some of the county's unemployed were absorbed in road-building crews and airport construction. In the fall of 1930, "with unemployment one of the greatest problems confronting the country, there [was] a gain in the number of men engaged in road building."[52] Nationwide it was estimated that in the number of men employed, the federal aid system resulted in a 4 percent increase over 1929.[53] Wyoming and Sweetwater County benefitted from the increased amount of monies spent on road improvements. Rock Springs also benefitted from the expenditure of funds used to improve the regional airport. Since the town was one of the stops along the route of the first transcontinental air mail line, the city had always benefitted from private and federal funds spent on improving air mail services. In 1930, forty thousand dollars was spent on a combination hangar and administration building that would contain enough space for "tri-motored planes, shops, ticket, radio, and weather service offices."[54] Road improvements and construction of new facilities at the airport

(Top) Automobile repair shop in Rock Springs in the 1920s. Courtesy of the New Studio, Rock Springs.

(Bottom) A delivery truck in front of McCurtain Motors, Rock Springs, in the 1920s. Courtesy of the New Studio, Rock Springs.

(Top) The interior of the Rialto Theatre in Rock Springs on February 28, 1921. Area residents attended plays or movies at the Rialto. Courtesy of the New Studio, Rock Springs.

(Bottom) Entertainment in Rock Springs, June 24, 1921. Courtesy of the New Studio, Rock Springs.

helped offset the loss of jobs, but they were seasonal construction jobs and did not replace jobs lost on the railroad.

The news for Sweetwater County unemployed grew worse in early 1931. The Central Coal and Coke Company Coal Mine in Rock Springs closed. As a result, seventy-five miners were laid off. Managers hoped the mine would reopen in three or four months. They also speculated that "a number of the men affected by the layoff are in the habit of following other pursuits than coal mining during the spring months and believed many of the 75 [would] find other employment."[55] In reality, the possibility of finding employment in the midst of the Depression was not good.

People's personal perceptions of the effect the Depression had on their lives is varied. Hugh Crouch, a black coal miner who worked at the Dines Mine north of Rock Springs, felt that the depression had pendulum swings between good and bad times. Crouch states: "in the early thirties, it was pretty bad." But at times "you could still get $1 a day," if the coal mines were working.[56] Yet there were too many periods of time when the mines did not operate. Crouch recalls: "there were several years there where we just drifted along. I don't know how we did it. When you eat everything in the house today and don't know what you're going to eat tomorrow, why you [are] just drifting along."[57] To help feed his family, Hugh Crouch hunted wild game. He remembered that: "We hunted and fished mostly the year round. We didn't have a season. . . . I guess they had a season, but we ignored it. When it comes to survival, you're not going to worry too much if it's season or not."[58]

Sweetwater County slowly began to emerge from the depression in the late 1930s. This slow recovery came about due to two factors. First, federal funds administered by the Civilian Conservation Corps (CCC) and the Works Progress Administration (WPA) greatly boosted the area's economy. Two CCC camps were located in the county during the depression. One was on the banks of the Green River; the other in the Eden Valley. Revenues in the form of wages and government contracts to provide services to these camps provided a needed infusion of capital into the local economy. Secondly, Union Pacific Railroad and Coal Companies took advantage of depressed wages and costs to initiate much-needed upgrading of their facilities and equipment. At Reliance, for example, they built a state-of-the-art coal loading facility. This steel coal tipple, built in 1936, provided local construction contractors with much needed work.[59] Elsewhere at Superior, Union Pacific opened the D. O. Clark Coal Mine in 1937 and completely equipped it with modern machinery. It was one of the first underground mines in the state to rely entirely on machinery for mining and hauling coal to the surface.[60]

It would take the onset of World War II for the Depression to end. The fateful bombing of Pearl Harbor on December 7, 1941 forever altered the West. As elsewhere, it had a profound effect on Sweetwater County. At the time, the locomotives used by Union Pacific Railroad were primarily steam powered. The steam was heated by coal. Moreover, the war in the Pacific required a massive amount of men and material be shipped to the West Coast. Much of that traffic passed over the mainline through Green River and Rock Springs. With the onset of the war in the Pacific, trains ran day and night, and coal mines operated twenty-four hours a day. Many of those employed to insure that enough coal was produced were women.

In the recently-built tipple at Reliance, women sorted the coal. On picking tables they separated stone from coal. It was dusty, dirty, demanding work and many even contracted "black lung," a disease common to coal miners. Ultimately, the women of Sweetwater County made a major contribution to the war effort. They also helped Union Pacific Coal Company produce more coal from its Sweetwater County mines than it had ever produced before in its history. Amy Pivik recalls: "What I remember [most about World War II is] the women were working picking bony at the mines and working the filling stations. I don't remember the wages being that good."[61] Women also worked at the loading docks on the railroad.[62]

In addition to employing women, Union Pacific actively recruited

Interior of the Grand Theater, Rock Springs, June 24, 1921. Courtesy of the New Studio, Rock Springs.

workers from Oklahoma and Arkansas. Called "Okies and Arkies," these men and their families were faced with the difficulties most people who moved to Sweetwater County found during a boom. There was not enough housing and families often had to live in substandard homes. Antone Pivik and Mike Duzik, who worked in and around mines much of their lives, stated they were promised good jobs if they moved to Superior or Dines or one of the other coal camps. Union Pacific reportedly "loaded them up on trains and hauled them" to Sweetwater County. The Company told them they would not have to do any manual labor, and that the mines are all mechanized.[63] Of course, even in mechanized mines, shoveling coal was still important, and many quickly learned how to shovel coal or hand-sort bony in a tipple.

The boom in the coal industry did not last much past the end of World War II. By the early 1950s, Union Pacific Railroad began converting to diesel powered locomotives. Coal powered engines were slowly phased out and by the 1960s, Union Pacific had aban-

This photograph dated May 17, 1922, was taken during the Stock Growers Convention in Rock Springs. Courtesy of the New Studio, Rock Springs.

doned its operations in Superior, Dines, Reliance, and Rock Springs.[64] Frank Dernovich tells a typical story of what happened when the Union Pacific coal mines laid a miner off due to closing down the operation. Dernovich stated: "[W]hen the mines closed, that's when I went out to Quealy." The Quealy coal mines were south of Rock Springs. From Quealy, Dernovich went to work in the newly-opened trona mines at Food Machinery Corporation (FMC).[65] Eugene Paoli had a similar experience. He recalls, "I was on starvation wages. You know, you got three kids, and you're not working." He could find one job—wages were low but "it was the only place [I] could find a job, before [I] went out to Westvaco [FMC]." Paoli states it clearly: "It was tough."[66] For coal miners who lost their jobs, the trona mines were lifesavers. Whether working beneath the ground to mine coal, or "digging out" trona, the miners sought the wealth of the county that lay below the ground. For most of its history, Sweetwater County had depended on the buried deposits of natural gas, oil, coal and now it was fortunate to possess within its boundaries one of the richest deposits of "soda" in the world.

The world's largest deposits of trona are located west of the Green River. Sweetwater County is home to five major processing facilities and mines that extract this material. Trona is a resource that has numerous applications. Primarily used in glass manufacturing, soda ash is also important in soap, detergent, water treatment, paper pulp production, photography, and in petroleum refining. Eventually, FMC (1948-1950), Rhone Poulenc (Stauffer), (1962), Allied Chemical (1965), Texasgulf (1975), and Tenneco (1982), would open plants in Sweetwater County and together they account for 90 percent of all the soda ash produced in the United States.

While the presence of trona had long been known, the credit for the formal discovery of the trona beds now being mined belongs to Mountain Fuel Supply Company. In the late 1930s, Mountain Fuel discovered, in drilling for natural gas, "mineral trona, a form of natural sodium carbonate."[67] FMC, which originally stood for Food Machinery Corporation, would open their mines near the Mountain Fuel discovery. Since FMC began mining in 1948, they have continuously expanded their operations. The mine covers over "24 square miles" and has "2,000 miles of tunnels."[68] As the other

(Top) Baseball games between the coal camps at Rock Springs, Superior, Cumberland (Lincoln County), and Hanna (Carbon County) took place every summer. This July 3, 1922, photograph shows the Hanna team in Rock Springs. Courtesy of the New Studio, Rock Springs.

(Bottom) The people of Sweetwater County placed a great deal of emphasis on education. Many came from immigrant families and saw education as the path to upward mobility. This photograph of Roosevelt School in Rock Springs dates to 1922. Courtesy of the New Studio, Rock Springs.

111

Uyeda family on K Street, September 3, 1922. Courtesy of the New Studio, Rock Springs.

trona mines came into existence, they too expanded their operations. In 1950, Wyoming's trona production stood at 29,658 tons; in 1990, it climbed to 16,231,257 tons. The valuation of this resource in 1990 was $179,369,884.[69] The primary use for trona is in glass manufacturing which accounts for about 55 percent of the consumption. The chemical industry consumes 23 percent; soap, 5 percent; pulp and paper manufacturing, 4 percent; 3 percent goes to water treatment. The remainder is shipped from Sweetwater County to be used in a variety of manners.[70] Currently, trona and natural gas production are among the county's leading sources of revenue.

In 1991, Sweetwater County had the second highest tax valuation in the state of Wyoming, standing at 773 million dollars.[71] For 1991, coal and natural gas had the highest valuation.[72] The third largest producer of oil in the county produced 8,265,000 barrels.[73] Coal was valued, for tax purposes, at $190,616,500; natural gas, $185,446,509; trona, $179,369,884; and oil, $177,714,287.

The opening of the trona mines greatly enriched Sweetwater County. Along with opening of the "trona patch," the expansion of the natural gas industry and the opening of both Bridger Coal and Black Butte Coal mines increased the prosperity of Sweetwater County in the 1970s. Mountain Fuel, Wexpro, Questar, and Union Pacific Resources all continued to tap into the area's rich natural gas fields at an accelerated pace. In many ways, Mountain Fuel and the other natural gas operations were among the county's most stable companies. Since the 1920s, natural gas firms have employed Sweetwater County workers. Families were raised in their "man camps" at Hiawatha, Clay Basin, Mullen Camp, and Powder Wash just south of the state line in Colorado. All of these camps were owned by Mountain Fuel Company.

Early on, the natural gas companies decided to build camps to house workers. Mountain Fuel employed maintenance crews to monitor wells and pipelines in remote corners of the county. Many of the men had families and the company built homes to accommodate them. For children growing up in these camps, life consisted of freedom to roam and play across the desert. Kathy Gilbert, who spent part of her childhood at Hiawatha, proclaimed "the greatest danger was rattlesnakes, but these could be avoided." Gilbert recalls her childhood with fondness. Growing up in a natural gas camp was one of the unique experiences of having parents who worked for Mountain Fuels. It was also a part of growing up in Wyoming."[74] Naturally, others viewed the "man camps" differently, but overall, if one could tolerate the isolation and distances from services, the communities were viewed favorably. There were those, however, who detested the isolation and found the long winters intolerable and the small communities confining.

As history inches closer to the present, it is often difficult to discuss what is taking place, particularly because everyone views occurrences through their own eyes, and also because of the complexity of the events is apparent to more people. Things are not as simple as they often seem to be in printed texts. Most historians look to the past hoping they can predict the future, but know full well they cannot. Yet, when Black Butte Coal announced it would lay off two hundred miners by March of 1993, historical precedents were in place.[75] Mines open and mines close. Coal contracts are won and lost and the company that loses either has to find another contract or face closing the mine. Two factors are in operation. First, economics, or the market, determine how much coal is needed and what the price per ton will be. Second, resources can be exhausted. Coal seams pinch out and it may not be profitable to move elsewhere to keep the mine open. Thus, due to economics and limited resources, mines close. In fact, there has

(Top) First Baptist Church Sunday School class in Rock Springs on July 27, 1922. Courtesy of the New Studio, Rock Springs.

(Bottom) Anderson house and store at 114 West Flat in Rock Springs, October 19, 1922.

This is a 1923 photograph of the Sunada family. George (age four) is on the tricycle; Edith (age two) is on the horse; Mary (age five), Marijivo (father); Toku (mother) and Tom Sunada (uncle) are also shown here.

never been a mine opened that did not close. That is obvious and may seem trite to say. It is something like saying, "it is dark in the desert at night." Yet, sometimes the obvious needs to be remembered, because by taking precautions, or remembering a flashlight at night, it is easier to travel through the dark. Knowing that mines close is important in planning the future—a future that is better illuminated by facts from the past may be easier to face. Too many people lightly regard the fact that minerals become exhausted and that when they are depleted or markets change, mines close. The desert has recaptured many who failed to see ahead. The land is scarred with trails, lined with graves, and marked by empty, abandoned mines. The environment reclaims human errors leaving traces of the past on the land. The scars are seen on the soil and in stones of the desert. The desert winds carry bits of this scarred earth in the sands it carries across time. For as long as anyone has written about or photographed the desert, the winds and sand have blown against the carcasses of empty buildings and abandoned homes.

It is also good to remember the spirit with which Rock Springs and Green River have continued. The desert also carries the marks

Japanese show on Mikado Day (or emperor's birthday) taken in Rock Springs, August 2, 1928. Courtesy of the New Studio, Rock Springs.

of success. Some thought in the 1950s, when the coal mines closed, that Rock Springs was destined to become a ghost town. Not even South Superior, which most onlookers thought certainly would vanish in 1963, when D. O. Clark closed, disappeared. Why did the people not just leave? Some did leave, but many stayed because of their ties to the land. The past shows that for over seven thousand years humans have lived in southwestern Wyoming. For as long as there have been written records, the life cycle of birth and death have occurred in this desert. In relation to the rest of the nation, the area has always been underpopulated, but it has never been void of inhabitants since the end of the last Ice Age. A land that is scarcely populated is part of the area's history. There were fewer Eastern Shoshoni in Wyoming than there were, say for example, Cherokees, in similar sized areas in the southeast United States.[76] Comparing our prehistoric population to other parts of North America demonstrates continuity in our past. Relatively low populations in comparison to the other areas has been the norm. It is nothing new that in relationship to the rest of North America, the population is sparse. Based on the 1990 Census, Wyoming is currently the least populated state in the nation. In fact, that may be the beauty of this remote place in southwestern Wyoming—we have what Gretel Ehrlich calls the *Solace of Open Spaces*.[77]

(Top) Rock Spring's "Union Special Shoe Shop," November 25, 1927. Courtesy of the New Studio, Rock Springs.

(Bottom) Saints Cyril and Methodius Catholic Church in Rock Springs on December 15, 1925. Courtesy of the New Studio, Rock Springs.

(Top) Loading coal at the Lionkol Mine north of Rock Springs in October of 1926. Courtesy of the New Studio, Rock Springs.

(Bottom) Reliance was a coal town owned and controlled by Union Pacific Coal Company, photograph 1928. Courtesy of the New Studio, Rock Springs.

The "First Broadway Restaurant" in Wamsutter, Wyoming, was built prior to 1928. It was intended to take advantage of traffic on U.S. 30 (the Old Lincoln Highway).

"Ferguson Mercantile Branch Store" built in 1907 at Wamsutter. Sheepman of the area were stockholders. "Jim Hanson and John Ferguson built the stone living quarters [which] were in the rear as were warehouses and barns for horses and wagons."

Lincoln Market chickens being fed in Rock Springs in July 1929. Courtesy of the New Studio, Rock Springs.

Chris Bunning, mayor, 1935; this mover and shaper of future Rock Springs was born March 14, 1859. He helped change Rock Springs and was a progressive mayor, bringing parks and better services to the city.

(Top) The Green River Soda Plant, circa 1930. Courtesy of the Wyoming State Archives, Cheyenne, J. E. Stimpson Collection.

(Bottom) Sweetwater Brewing Company at Green River in 1934.

(Top) Construction crews at the Rock Springs airport in 1934.
Courtesy of the New Studio, Rock Springs.

(Bottom) Joe Bozovich, a coal miner and later archaeologist, with
his airplane in 1933. Rock Springs was located on the first transcontinental air mail route in the United States and served as an
important stop for the air route.

Naturalization class in Rock Springs, circa 1910s to 1920s. Courtesy of the New Studio, Rock Springs.

Logan's Ranch School was in District No. 3, located on Sage Creek south of Rock Springs. This photograph was taken in 1930.

Oddfellows band in a 1935 parade. Taken in front of Northside State Bank at the corner of North Front and K Street, in Rock Springs. Courtesy of the New Studio, Rock Springs.

"The graduating class of 1936" from the Wyoming General Hospital in Rock Springs.

This is the "interior" of Green River's Oxford Club in 1937. Courtesy of the New Studio, Rock Springs.

A section foreman's house at Point of Rocks. Few of these remain in Wyoming. In the 1930s, section foremen for this railroad camp were Japanese.

Few section houses are left standing in Wyoming. This one, at Point of Rocks, housed railroad repairmen. At the turn of the century, most section crews were Japanese. After World War II, the majority were of Hispanic descent.

(Top) The coal town of Winton, circa 1930s. The large building in the center is Union Pacific's company store.

(Bottom) Aerial photograph of Rock Springs, note the viaduct over the railroad is not yet complete. This was printed by Union Pacific Company in one of their promotional pamphlets. Some historic buildings in Chinatown and at Camp Pilot Butte are still standing. (Photograph not dated.)

The interior of Reliance
No. 7 Mine in May 1939.

The Reliance tipple in 1936.

"Picking tables inside the Reliance Tipple in 1936."

The opening of the D. O. Clark mine at Superior in 1937.

One of the first coal cars in the D. O. Clark mine at Superior in 1937.

Inside of the Civilian Conservation Corps (CCC) canteen at Green River in 1938.

Civilian Conservation Corps camp in 1938.

Group at an Elks' parade in Rock Springs. (Photograph not dated)

(Top) Rock Springs "male chorus," March 1, 1941.   *(Bottom) At Table Rock, the discovery of oil led to the creation of this small community. Located along Interstate 80, the small community housed oil field workers and a gas processing plant.*

"Mrs. Margaret Henneck, acting postmistress" stands in front of the post office at Wamsutter. Her daughter Bobbie is seated. (Photograph not dated)

The Rialto Theatre, Rock Springs, opened in February 1921 and closed in April 1959. It was a primary source of entertainment in Rock Springs.

Jane Hanni worked as a slate-picker in the tipples at Superior in 1943. "Bony pickers," as they were called, were faced with the dusty, dirty job of separating stone from coal inside these coal loading and sorting facilities called "tipples."

A snow storm in 1949 stranded trucks in Rock Springs. Such occurrences continue today during winter snows.

Sweetwater County homestead. (Photograph not dated.)

"First Jury with women who tried a criminal case: State vs. Lang," May 9, 1950. Front row, left to right, Donna Schultz (Reliance), Kathryn Auld (Reliance), Mrs. John Wilde (Rock Springs), Mrs. Dave Rauzi (Rock Springs), Mrs. Louise Graf (Jury foreman), Merton Schutz (Green River). Back row, left to right, Mrs. Dar Marshall (Rock Springs), Rank Parton (Thirteenth Juror, Rock Springs), Hugh Sweeney (South of Rock Springs), Bill Wonnacott (Rock Springs), Floyd Henry (Farson), and Alva Qualls (Superior).

Ranching and sheepherding dominate Sweetwater County's landscape.

Loading wool at the Mathew Ranch in 1925.

*"Darley's Sheep Crossing at Green River circa 1910."
Courtesy of the Sweetwater County Museum, E. H. Gaensslen Collection.*

Sheep do well on the arid steppe of southwestern Wyoming. Herders and their dogs dot the landscape and demonstrate continuity with the last century when ranching was first introduced to Wyoming.

Basque, Spanish, and Mexican herders worked tending sheep throughout Sweetwater County. Even today, the sheep industry is a major source of revenue in the area. Sheepherder wagons like these are still used as mobile homes on the range.

A hay rack in the Eden Valley. Stacking hay has often been accomplished with homemade equipment.

Winter on the ranch.

The Taliaferro Ranch in the Eden Valley. Linda Taliaferro is currently a County Commissioner. She, along with her husband Tom, are shown here during "haying" season.

Eden Pilot Farm, 1966 photograph.

Dragging the fields in the Eden Valley to prepare them for planting and irrigation.

Homemade haystacker in the Eden Valley.

The Farson store and its famed ice cream cones attract travelers and locals alike.

"Calving" in the spring consumes much of the ranch family's time. Since the newborn calves represent the future they are tended with loving care.

Maxon Ranch and the Clark family south of Rock Springs in 1992. Alex Clark, father; Jan Hilstad, his daughter; Jan's children, Erica, 15; Cody, 5; and Sage, 3.

Preparing to blast the "face" at Stansbury. The explosive will be "tamped" lightly into the hole and a "powder dummy" will be placed over the dynamite prior to blasting.

Quealy strip mine south of Rock Springs, Wyoming, circa 1950s.

The Gunn-Quealy (also called Rainbow) Coal Company was one of the first strip mines in Sweetwater County. It was located south of Rock Springs.

This shows the thickness of the coal seam mined at Stansbury by the Union Pacific Coal Company.

Tamping in the explosives prior to blasting at Stansbury, 1952.

In spite of Stansbury being a mechanized mine, coal mining still required much manual labor; this photograph dates to 1952.

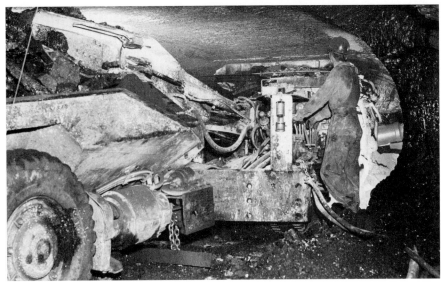

Setting roof supports inside the Stansbury mine in 1952.

Goodman miner used in the Stansbury Coal Mine during 1952.

Inside the D. O. Clark Mine at Superior in the 1950s.

A point of pride and necessity was safety in the mines. This sign shows how long the Stansbury mine worked without an accident.

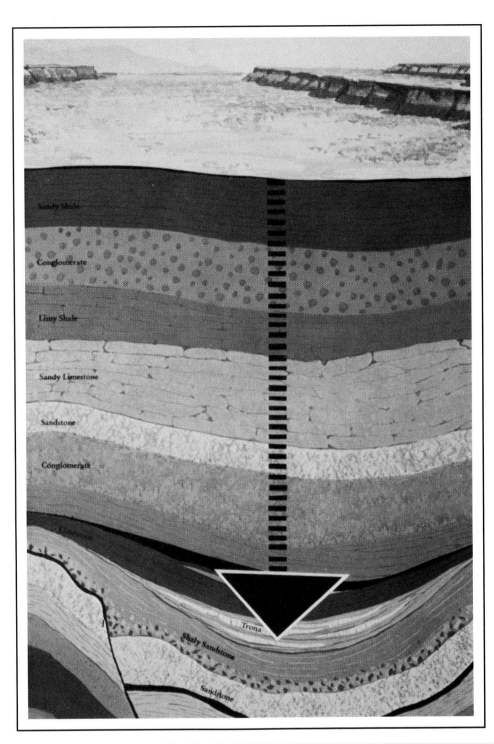

Sandy Shale

Conglomerate

Limy Shale

Sandy Limestone

Sandstone

Conglomerate

Limestone

Trona

Shaly Sandstone

Sandstone

This diagram shows the geological strata that overlies the trona beds at the Food Machinery Corporation (FMC) mine west of Green River.

Reliance No. 7 miners completed their fifth year without a lost-time injury, accumulating 2,055,131 man-hours. Photograph taken in 1952.

FMC soda ash plant west of Green River.

Trona miners have excavated hundreds of miles of tunnels under the Green River Basin using equipment such as this "Marrieta Borer Miner." From the FMC Mine Collection.

Diesel jeeps transport miners and foremen to the face, or working area, in the trona mines (FMC Mine). The tunnels form a complex underground network of passageways leading to past and present mining areas. Thousands of miles of tunnels exist at the mines. An hour ride to the working face by a crew of miners is often commonplace.

Longwall mining techniques, modified and borrowed from coal mining, cuts the trona deposits from between one foot to eighteen inches each time it passes along the wall of trona. The men are standing under the hydraulic roof supports. Only maintenance men are allowed on the other side of the machine. From the FMC Mine Collection, information Courtesy Henry Kovach.

Here the cutting tips of a "Marrietta Borer Miner" are being replaced by a maintenance worker. From the FMC Mine Collection.

This machine is known as a "Joy or Ripper Miner" sometimes called a "bore miner." It is also called a "Drum miner." It cuts into the top of the face, then downward. The face is the surface of the unmined trona deposits. Trona mining is highly mechanized; but the workers who operate the equipment are essential to smooth production. From the FMC Mine Collection.

Underground miners and equipment repairmen are the backbone of the trona industry in Sweetwater County.

Betty Ng teaching her class in Rock Springs District No. 1. Born in Hong Kong, Betty Ng is a naturalized U.S. citizen. She continues the tradition of fine education in Sweetwater County Schools. Courtesy of Paul Ng.

The Sweetwater County tradition of quality education continues at Western Wyoming College. The college was paid for through a bond issue approved by citizens of Sweetwater County.

Aerial view of Green River, 1990s.

Placing the Christmas tree at Green River, December 11, 1984. Courtesy of The Green River Star.

The Eden Valley has a rich
farming and ranching tradition.
The communities of Eden and
Farson serve the surrounding
area with the essentials of life,
including beer.

Farson cafe located adjacent to
the Oregon/Mormon/Pioneer Trail.

Creston Junction's "Outlaw Junction Bar" is located along the route of the transcontinental railroad, historic Lincoln Highway, U.S. 30, and Interstate 80.

The interior of Creston Junction Bar, 1992.

(Top) Sweetwater County's rich natural gas reserves are among the largest in the nation.

(Bottom) The "drilling rigs" become miniature villages equipped with their own generators and oftentimes have bunk houses and cooking facilities to accommodate the workers.

This Sinclair station at Creston Junction was built to serve interstate travelers. Built along U.S. 30, the station's above-ground storage tank, small building size, and architecture are representative of a past period when full service and two-lane roads were the norm.

Ferguson Mercantile at Wamsutter in 1992.

In the last century, railroads served as the main routes east and west.
Now, the Interstate Highway serves that function. Due to weather
extremes, repairing roads is an annual event. Folklore has it that you
can tell it is springtime in Wyoming when the back hoes come out.

Street scene in Green River, Wyoming, in 1992.

Wamsutter had its beginning around 1868. It was built to serve the railroad. Today, the town provides services for oil field workers. In the last decade, it served a thriving uranium industry north of town.

The Wamsutter water tower is a reminder of an era when locomotives were powered by steam.

Sale of fireworks provide another form of income at Creston Junction.

During the "boom" of the 1970s and early 1980s, trailers served as a first home for most Rock Springs residents.

False fronts on buildings like this one in Wamsutter purposefully reflect a building tradition that goes back to the 1800s.

The legacy of the past.

South Superior, Wyoming is all that remains of a once-large coal community consisting of Superior, A Camp, B Camp, C Hill, C Camp, Copenhagen, D Camp, Premier, and a few houses near D. O. Clark. The communities had their beginnings in the first decade of the 1900s but by 1963, the large mines had closed, leaving only a few remnants of a once-thriving community.

South Superior town hall. South Superior was the set for a recent Meg Tilly movie, Leaving Normal.

(Opposite page) The Rock Springs City Hall, built from locally quarried sandstone, was constructed in the early 1890s. Recently restored, this civic building reflects the craftsmanship and skill of local stonemasons.

The Chilton Mine located north of Rock Springs was a small, locally owned and operated coal mine. Such mines provided fuel for homes and cash for ranchers, like the Chiltons.

(Top) The Chilton Coal Mine north of Boar's Tusk.

(Bottom) The Reliance Tipple, 1990.

169

The Brewery at Green River.

The United Mine Workers' union hall at South Superior was built in the early 1920s using union dues and donations.

This coal miner's home at Superior was built entirely from railroad ties.

Rock Springs in the 1980s.

Shotgun houses in Rock Springs were built by coal companies to house miners. A few of these turn-of-the-century buildings were modified and by the boom of the 1970s, they served as homes for a new wave of miners.

The unique nature of the homes in Rock Springs is due to several factors. One, emigrants from around the world built homes similar to those in Europe; two, the coal companies dictated how homes were to be built; and three, the constant reuse and modification of buildings first constructed at an outlying mine camp, then later moved into Rock Springs when the camp was abandoned.

Along this highway, in front of "Grub's," passed first Overland Stagecoaches, then trucks and cars on the Lincoln Highway, and finally, auto traffic on U.S. 30.

Signs of the present show Rock Springs as a late twentieth-century American town; yet, the coal cart in the foreground shows the roots in the past. The contrast between old and new is evident in the wooden cart and plastic neon signs.

Trailers and Interstate 80 both reflect the continuity of boom and bust and people passing through. The concept behind both is mobility.

Continuity marks the history of Green River. From the first wood-fired train that arrived in 1868, to today's diesel engines, railroading has been a way of life for generations of residents living in this town.

The Beckwith and Quinn store is the place where the Chinese miners bought their goods in the nineteenth century. Beckwith and Quinn held all the labor contracts for the Chinese. This building along with other pieces of the past have vanished, but the landscape surrounding Rock Springs remains much the same.

The remains of the Copenhagen tipple north of South Superior. Tipples were used to sort, then load, coal into waiting railroad cars.

Walking path over the railroad yards. The riveted iron shows the work of craftsmen. Ironworking is a craft that is slowly disappearing.

(Opposite page) The cemetery at Superior reflects the ethnic diversity of the mining camp. Headstones were written in Italian, Japanese, or English, and provide clues to the origins of the town's inhabitants.

In southwestern Wyoming, uncluttered horizons and limitless vistas shape much of what people think about the region. Sweetwater County's Red Desert is one area where neither fences or power poles interrupt the landscape.

Children's graves made up most of the burials in many mining camp cemeteries. This photograph shows the cemetery at Superior.

Various groups in Rock Springs including Slovenians, Finns, and Italians had associations or clubs that meet on a regular basis. This photograph shows one such group circa 1910–1920.

Gunn Mine east of Rock Springs, not dated, but circa 1910-1920. Courtesy of the New Studio, Rock Springs.

Storefront in Rock Springs. "Fine Candies, Ice Cream and Soda Water" were sold here; during prohibition, many soda water shops sold alcohol.

Wagon in front of a stone house at Rock Springs. (Photograph not dated)

Conclusion

One cannot escape the landscape. Nor is it even desirable for the knowledgeable to want to alter this land of endless sky and moving sands. One can bulldozer-blade the sands, but the land is marked forever. Rock Art and trail ruts still visible from the 1800s prove that humans leave marks that last for decades and centuries. There are no forests to hide the marks, no season-long rains to erode away the sandstone and blot away the marks of Native Americans. And in some ways, the manmade marks become the landscape, part of a new environment, and they become as mysterious and beautiful as a soaring hawk above tan sandstone cliffs—the bird marking an otherwise cloudless sky, the cliffs cutting sharp edges against a deep blue background.

There are still great spaces between towns in Sweetwater County. Green River and Rock Springs are laced together in a loose knot of shared landscape and the familiarity of intense competition, but beyond these two towns the distance between tiny villages and scattered homes is great. North and south of Interstate 80 vast reaches stretch for hundreds of miles. Like Mary Austin wrote about the Owens Valley, in the shadow of the Sierra Madres, the nature of the land insures it will not be lived in except on its own terms. The Shoshonis who lived here lived like the trees, with great spaces between each plant.[1] People in Sweetwater County live like this also for they have wide expanses between their towns.

Wallace Stegner says the true western town exists in the "boon docks where the interstates do not reach. . . ."[2] It seems this applies to Rock Springs and Green River, even though there is a college and the ubiquitous McDonalds. These towns are islands in a sea of open expanses. As Stegner notes, true western towns have roads that lead into them "out of wide emptiness," then they thread through "a

---

*Sweet's Bar and Cafe located at the "Section Camp of Kanda."
Approximately every six miles along the Union Pacific Railroad there were section camps. These camps were moved often. Between Rock Springs and Green River, the camps of Carmichael (built in 1868), Wilkens, then Kanda served crews repairing the rails. The repair crews at Rock Springs, Kanda, and Green River worked long hours to insure the tracks remained in good condition.*

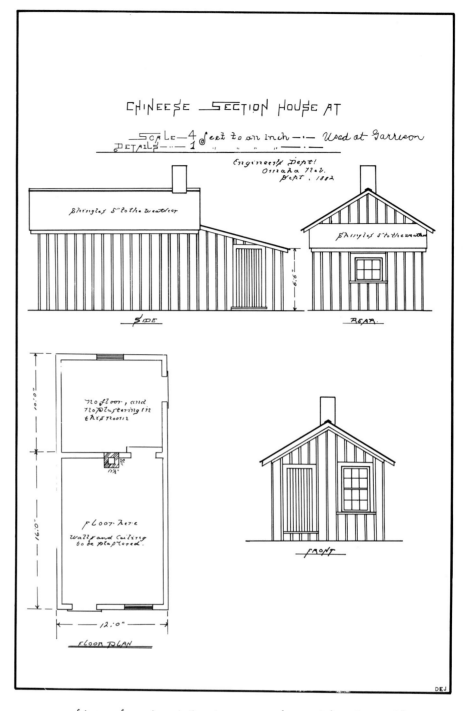

CHINEESE SECTION HOUSE AT

SCALE — 4 feet to an inch — Used at Garrison
DETAILS — 1 " " " " "

Engineer's Dept!
Omaha Neb.
Sept. 1882

Shingles 5" to the weather

SIDE

Shingles 5" to the weather

REAR

no floor, and
no plastering in
this room

floor here
walls and ceiling
to be plastered.

FRONT

FLOOR PLAN

DEJ

Union Pacific Railroad and Coal Company built houses of the same size for all Chinese workers whether they were in coal or section camps. In Rock Springs today, these are still evident. Note that the architect misspelled Chinese.

fringe of service station taverns, and a motel or two, widens to a couple of blocks of commercial buildings, some still false-fronted, with glimpses of side streets' green lawns." The road, according to Stegner, then "narrows to another strip of automotive roadside, and disappears into more wide emptiness."[3] One need only drive south on Wyoming 430 in Rock Springs and past the industry on the edge of town to see this world described by Stegner. Or drive north on U.S. 191 through Farson and the world of Stegner emerges. The West is Sweetwater County with its mines, cowboys, river runners, trappers, traders, women, and emigrants who have passed over the same landscape to the present.

Union Pacific Railroad Crew, 1936. Left to Right are: Paul Murray, brakeman; Gordon Graham, brakeman, Dale J. Morris, brakeman, Robert Alpin, fireman; Edward Lewis, engineer.

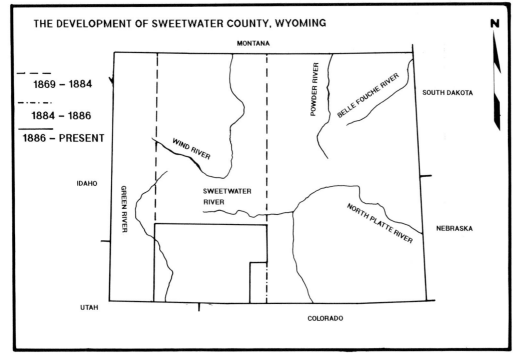

In 1869, Sweetwater County ran from the Utah/Colorado border to Montana. The northern border was moved south to its present location in the mid-1880s. Later, Carbon County gained the southeast corner and when Wyoming became a state, the county looked like it does today. In the late nineteenth century, the county assumed its present configuration. In area, the county is roughly the state of Connecticut.

The shifting sands in the Killpecker Dune field stretch from north of Rock Springs to the Platte River in Carbon County. Although not very wide, the dune field is well over one hundred miles long, and dotted with pools of water formed by melting winter ice and snow covered by drifting sands.

Chapter Notes

Preface and Acknowledgments

1. A. Delano, *Life on the Plains and Among the Diggings Being Scenes and Adventures of an Overland Journey to California* (New York: Time Life reprint of 1854 edition, 1981), 119-120.

2. Bruce L. McKinstry, *The California Gold Rush Overland Diary of Bryan N. McKinstry 1850-1852* (Glendale, California: The Arthur H. Clark Co., 1975), 180.

Introduction

1. For a discussion of Mormon pioneers on the Overland Trail, see A. Dudley Gardner, Debbie Allen, and Mike Allen, "The Washakie Stage Station," Ms. on file at the Rawlins District Office of the Bureau of Land Management, District Archaeologist Office. The report is also on file at the Archeological Service of Western Wyoming College.

Chapter I

1. Paul C. Phillips, ed., *Warren Angus Ferris: A Diary of the Wanderings and Sources of the Rivers Missouri, Columbia, and Colorado from February 1830 to November, 1835: Life in the Rocky Mountains* (Denver: Old West Publishing Co., 1940), 126.

2. Brigham D. Madsen, *Exploring the Great Salt Lake: The Stansbury Expedition of 1840-50* (Salt Lake City: University of Utah Press, 1987), 639.

3. Fred R. Gowans, *Rocky Mountain Rendezvous: A History of the Fur Trade Rendezvous 1825-1840* (Layton, Utah: Peregrine Smith, 1985), 18.

4. *Ibid.*

5. *Ibid.*, 106-7.

6. *Ibid.*, 113.

7. *Ibid.*

8. *Ibid.*, 115.

9. Madsen, *Exploring the Great Salt Lake,* 632.

10. Fred R. Gowans and Eugene E. Campbell, *Fort Bridger: Island in the Wilderness* (Provo: Brigham Young University Press, 1975), 8.

11. *Ibid.*, 10.

12. *Ibid.*

13. *Ibid.*

14. Doyce B. Nunis ed., *The Bidwell-Bartleson Party 1841 California Emigrant Adventure, The Documents and Memoirs of the Overland Pioneers* (Santa Cruz, California: Tanager Press, 1991), 1.

15. *Ibid.*, 8-9.

16. John W. Caughey ed., *California,* rev. ed., (Englewood Cliffs, New Jersey: Prentice Hall, 1959), 213.

17. Nunis, *The Bidwell-Bartleson Party,* 8. The Bidwell diary points out some of these concerns after they were well into present Nevada.

18. *The New Yorker,* September 28, 1992, 28.

19. Nunis, *The Bidwell-Bartleson Party,* 42, 43, 47-50.

20. *Ibid.*, 245.

21. *Ibid.*, 246.

22. *Ibid.*, 169.

23. John D. Unruh. *Plains Across: The Overland Emigrants and the Trans-Mississippi West, 1840-60* (Urbana: University of Illinois Press, 1979), 157.

24. Donald Jackson and Mary Lee Spence, eds., *The Expeditions of John Charles Frémont, Volume 1, Travel from 1838 to 1844* (Urbana: University of Illinois Press, 1970), 475. Frémont makes several interesting points giving the history of how Green River was so named. He writes: "This is the emigrant road to Oregon which bears much to the southward to avoid the mountains about the western head of Green River—the Rio Verde of the Spaniards." He also notes that the Indian name for the Green River was Seeds Ke Dee Agie (466).

25. Edwin Bryant, *What I Saw in California, Being the Journal of a Traveler by the Emigrant Route and South Pass of the Rocky Mountains, Across the Continent of North America, the Great Basin, and Through California, In the Years 1846, 1947,* (Minneapolis: Ross and Hainer, 1967 reprint), 144-45.

26. Joel Palmer, *Journal of Travels over the Rocky Mountains to the Mouth of the Columbia River; Made During the Years 1845 and 1846* (Cincinnati: J. A. and U. P. James, 1847), 35.

27. In Dale Morgan, *Overland in 1846: Diaries and Letter of the California-Oregon Trail* (Georgetown, California: The Talisman Press, 1963), 127. William E. Taylor was bound for California via the Central Overland route.

28. *Ibid.*, 35.

29. Madsen, *Exploring the Great Salt Lake,* 632.

30. Dale L. Morgan ed., *The Overland Diary of James A. Pritchard from Kentucky to California in 1849* (Denver: Old West Publishing Co., 1959), 97.

31. Lewis Shutterly, *The Diary of Lewis Shutterly* (Saratoga, Wyoming: Saratoga Historical and Cultural Association, 1981), 26. Normally, the number used to estimate population by lodges is 4. Thus, 4 X 200 = 800 and thus Shutterly's estimate might be too high. Even at a higher rate of 6 Shoshoni per lodge, Shutterly's count may still be too great.

32. John Francis McDermott ed., *An Artist on the Overland Trail—1849 Diary and Sketching James F. Wilkins*

(San Marino, California: Huntington Library, 1968), 57.

33. Linda Scott Cummings, Paleo Research Laboratories, Golden, Colorado, personal communication August, 1992. A. Dudley Gardner and David E. Johnson, "Results of the 1992 Archaeological Excavations at Fort Bridger," (Rock Springs, Western Wyoming Community College, Archaeological Services, In prep.).

34. Bruce L. McKinstry, *The California Gold Rush Diary of Bryan N. McKinstry 1850-1852* (Glendale, California: Arthur H. Clark, Co., 1975), 193.

35. P. V. Crawford, "Journal of a Trip Across the Plains, 1851," *Quarterly of the Oregon Historical Society* 25 (June 1924), 147.

36. Bert Webber, ed., *The Oregon and Overland Trail Diary of Mary Louisa Black in 1865* (Medford, Oregon: Pacific Northwest Books Company, 1989), 45.

37. Green River City is the name given to present Green River in 1868.

38. *Eighth Census of the United States,* Green River Precinct, Territory of Utah, September 10, 1860, p. 325.

39. *Ibid.*

40. Randall H. Hewitt, *Across the Plains and Over the Divide: A Mule Train Journey from East to West in 1862, and Incidents Connected Therewith* (New York: Argosy - Antiquarian Ltd., 1964), 223-24.

41. *Ibid.,* 223.

42. *Ibid.,* 224.

43. A. Howard Cutting, "Journal of an Overland Trip 1863," manuscript on file at the Henry H. Huntington Library and Art Gallery, San Marino, California, Reprinted by permission of the Huntington Library. Reprint in: A. Dudley Gardner and D. E. Johnson, "Historic Overview of the Bitter Creek Valley from Rock Springs to Green River," *Cultural Resource Management Report No. 47* (Rock Springs: Archaeological Services of Western Wyoming College, 1988), Appendix A.

44. *Ibid.*

45. W. Settle and M. L. Settle, eds., *Overland Days to Montana in 1865, The Diary of Sarah Raymond and Journal of Dr. Waid Howard* (Glendale, California: Arthur H. Clark Company, 1971), 206.

46. *Ibid.*

Chapter II

1. For a discussion of the much talked about move from South Pass to Green River, see Ora E. Wright and Lenora S. Wright, *Our Valley Eden Valley, Wyoming* (Portland: Gann Publishing, 1987). It should be noted that Sweetwater County formally came into existence in 1869 as a border-to-border county. But in 1868 the framework for creating the five border-to-border counties was set in place.

2. T. H. Heuterman, *Moveable Type: Biography of Leigh R. Freeman* (Ames: Iowa State University Press, 1979), 52.

3. *Ibid.,* 27.

4. *Ibid.,* 26.

5. [Green River City] *Frontier Index,* August 11, 1868, p. 1.

6. *Ibid.,* September 1, 1868, p. 3.

7. *Ibid.,* September 18, 1868, p. 3.

8. *Ibid.,* October 13, 1868, p. 3.

9. *Ibid.,* September 25, 1868, p. 3.

10. *Ibid.,* September 29, 1868, p. 3.

11. *Ibid.,* August 28, 1868, p. 1.

12. *Ibid.,* November 3, 1868, p. 3.

13. *Ibid.*

14. *Ibid.*

15. A. Dudley Gardner, "The Overland Trail From Bridger's Pass to Fort Bridger," Manuscript on file, Archaeological Services of Western Wyoming College, Rock Springs, 115.

16. *Frontier Index,* July 3, 1868, p. 2.

17. *Ibid.,* September 22, 1868, p. 2.

18. *Ibid.,* September 1, 1868.

19. *Ibid.,* June 12, 1868, p. 3; July 3, 1868, p. 2.

20. *Ibid.*

21. *Ibid.,* September 22, 1868, p. 3.

22. *Ibid.,* August 28, 1868, p. 3.

23. *Ibid.,* September 29, 1868, p. 3.

24. *Ibid.,* September 22, 1868, p. 3.

25. Howard Stansbury, *Exploration and Survey of the Valley of the Great Salt Lake of Utah* (Washington: Robert Armstrong Printer, 1853), 234.

26. James A. Evans, "Report of James A. Evans of an Exploration from Camp Walbach to Green River, in 1865," Ms. on file, Union Pacific Historical Museum, File K-13-1, Omaha, Nebraska, 11.

27. *Frontier Index,* September 1, 1868, pp. 3, 12.

28. J. D. Hague and Clarence King, *Mining Industry, United States Geological Exploration of the Fortieth Parallel* (Washington: U.S. Government Printing Office, 1870), 472.

29. Silas Reed, *Report of Silas Reed, Surveyor General of Wyoming Territory for the Year 1871* (Washington: U.S. Government Printing Office, 1871), 21.

30. *Ibid.,* 20.

31. T. A. Larson, *History of Wyoming* (Lincoln: University of Nebraska Press, 1978), 113.

32. *Ibid.,* 114.

33. *Ibid.*

34. Wyoming Secretary of the Territory, *Resources of Wyoming: The Vacant Public Lands and How to Obtain Them* (Cheyenne: The Daily Sun Electric Print, 1889), 6. Hereafter cited *Resources of Wyoming 1889.*

35. *Resources of Wyoming 1889,* 65.

36. *Ibid.*

37. *Ibid.*

38. Louis D. Ricketts, *Annual Report of the Territorial Geologists to the Governor of Wyoming* (Cheyenne: Daily Leader Steam Book Print, 1890), 12-15.

39. *Ibid.*

40. Richard Reinhardt, *Our West on the Overland Train: Across-the-Continent Excursion and Leslie's Magazine in 1877 and the Overland Trip in 1967* (Palo Alto, California: The American West Publishing Company, 1968), 80.

41. *Ibid.,* 80-81.

42. *Ibid.,* 81.

43. *Ibid.,* 83.

44. Val Brinkerhoff and A. Dudley Gardner, *An American Place: A Centennial Portrait of Rock Springs Wyoming, Then and Now* (Rock Springs: Pioneer Press, Western Wyoming Community College, 1990), 33-34. Hereafter cited as *An American Place.* For census figures see *Ninth Census of the United States, 1870* (Washington: U.S. Government Printing Office, 1872); *Tenth Census of the United States, 1890* (Washington, D.C.: U.S. Government Printing Office, 1880); *Eleventh Census of the United States, 1890* (Washington: U.S. Government Printing Office, 1842).

45. *Ninth Census of the United States* (Washington: Government Printing Office, 1872).

46. *Ibid.*

47. "Mrs. Frank Leslie," *California: A Pleasure Trip from Gotham to the Golden Gate April, May, June 1877* (New York: Nieuwkoop and B. De Graaf Company, 1972), 203.

48. *Ibid.,* 203-5.

49. *An American Place,* 7.

50. A. Dudley Gardner and Verla R. Flores, *Forgotten Frontier: A History of Wyoming Coal Mining* (Boulder, Colorado: Westview Press 1989).

51. *An American Place,* 338.

52. *Ibid.*

53. Union Pacific Railway, *Resources and Attractions of Wyoming for the Home Seeker Capitalists and Tourist* (Saint Louis: Woodward and Tierum Printing, 1892), 80-81.

54. *An American Place,* 33.

55. *Ibid.,* 33-34.

56. *Ibid.,* 34.

57. *Ibid.,* 35. See *Twelfth Census of the United States, 1900* (Washington: U.S. Government Printing Office, 1901); and *Fourteenth Census of the United States, 1920* (Washington, D.C.: U.S. Government Printing Office, 1922).

58. *Cheyenne Daily Sun-Leader,* January 21, 1899, p. 1. See Jim William June, Marna Grubb and Ruth Lauritzen, *Self Guided Tour of Historical Green River* (Green River: Green River Historic Preservation Commission, 1991).

59. *Ibid.,* 36.

60. A. R Schultz, *The Northern Part of the Rock Springs Coal Field Sweetwater County, Wyoming: Investigations of the Coal Fields of Wyoming by the United States Geological Survey of 1907,* (Washington: U. S. Government Printing Office, 1908), 251.

61. *Ibid.*

62. *Ibid.*

63. *Ibid.,* 274-75.

64. J. A. Taff, E. W. Shaw, C. W. Washburne, E. G. Woodruff, E. E. Smith, M. W. Ball, and A. R. Shultz, *Investigations of the Coal Fields of Wyoming by the United States Geological Survey in 1907* (Washington: U. S. Government Printing Office, 1909), 277-78.

65. In A. D. Gardner and Robert Rosenberg, *Archeological and Historic Survey of 16 Mine Reclamation Sites in Uinta and Lincoln Counties, Wyoming* (Rock Springs: Archeological Services of Western Wyoming College, Cultural Resource Management Report No. 13), 220-21.

66. *Census of Wyoming* (Cheyenne: Office of the Census of the State of Wyoming, 1915). For a discussion of the development of railroads such as the Oregon Short Line in Sweetwater County, see Gardner and Flores, *Forgotten Frontier.*

Chapter III

1. U. S. Department of Commerce, Bureau of Census, *County and City Data Book 1988* (Washington: U.S. Government Printing Office, 1988).

2. Virginia Scharff, *Taking the Wheel: Women and the Coming of the Motor Age* (Albuquerque: University of New Mexico Press, 1992), 25.

3. *Ibid.,* 45.

4. *Ibid.,* 28, 112.

5. Ezra Emery to Mrs. D. M. Thayer, Rock Springs Wyoming, April 7, 1904. Ezra Emery, microfilm, Ms. on file, Western Wyoming College. Original on file, Wyoming State Archives, Cheyenne, Ezra Emery file.

6. *Cheyenne Daily Leader,* December "A.D." 1895, p. 2.

7. *Ibid.*

8. Stanford J. Layton, *To No Privileged Class* (Provo: Charles Redd Center for Western Studies, Brigham Young University, 1988), 23.

9. *Ibid.,* 24.

10. *Ibid.*

11. *Ibid.*

12. Elinore Pruitt Stewart, *Letters of a Woman Homesteader* (Lincoln: University of Nebraska Press, 1989), 215.

13. Layton, *To No Privileged Class,* 58.

14. *Ibid.*

15. *Ibid.*

16. *Ibid.*

17. Barbara Allen, *Homesteading the High Desert* (Salt Lake City: University of Utah Press, 1987), 12.

18. *Ibid.*

19. *Ibid.,* 124.

20. *The Rock Springs Rocket,* February 14, 1930, p. 1.

21. *Ibid.*

22. *Ibid.*

23. Eden Valley is fortunate to have had three excellent historians who have documented the development of ranching in this area. Ora and Lenora Wright and Linda Simnacher have generated excellent works describing the history of this valley. See Linda Simnacher, "Preserving Eden: A Contemporary Ranch in Western Wyoming" (Master's thesis, University of Wyoming, 1991), 21, 23, 25; Ora E. Wright and Lenora S. Wright, *Our Valley Eden Valley, Wyoming* (Portland: Gann Publishing, 1987).

24. *Ibid.*

25. *Ibid.*

26. Interview with Rose Teters Logan conducted by Shirley Black, Ms on file Archaeological Services of Western Wyoming College, transcript, 4.

27. *Ibid.,* 6.

28. *Rock Springs Rocket,* April 28, 1917, p. 1.

29. *Rock Springs Miner,* December 21, 1917, p. 1.

30. *Rock Springs Miner,* September 21, 1917, p. 1.

31. *Rock Springs Miner,* September 28, 1917, p. 1.

32. *Rock Springs Miner,* October 5, 1917, pp. 1, 5.

33. *Ibid.,* 6.

34. *Rock Springs Miner,* February 18, 1918, p. 1. Actually this included all men sent overseas during the World War I to this point.

35. *Rock Springs Miner,* April 5, 1918, p. 1.

36. *Rock Springs Miner,* February 1, 1918, p. 1.

37. *Ibid.*

38. *Rock Springs Miner,* February 15, 1918, p. 1.

39. *Rock Springs Miner,* April 12, 1918, p. 1.

40. *Rock Springs Miner,* August 16, 1918, p. 1.

41. *Rock Springs Miner,* April 19, 1918, p. 1.

42. *Rock Springs Miner,* April 10, 1918, p. 1.

43. Gardner and Flores, *Forgotten Frontier.*

44. A. Dudley Gardner and David E. Johnson, "Cultural Resource Inventory and Mitigation of Thirty-Seven Mine Reclamation Sites in Sweetwater County, Wyoming, Vol. II," *Cultural Resource Management Report No. 29* (Rock Springs: Archaeological Services Western Wyoming College, 1986), Appendix H, 35. Appendix H of this report contains 123 pages of oral interview transcripts. Hereafter all oral interviews in this volume abbreviated: CRM No. 29.

45. *Ibid.*

46. *Ibid.*

47. T. A. Larson, *Wyoming: A History* (Lincoln: University of Nebraska Press, 1978).

48. *The Rock Springs Rocket,* November 6, 1930, p. 1.

49. *The Rock Springs Rocket,* December 4, 1930, p. 1.

50. *Ibid.*

51. *Ibid.*

52. [Rock Springs] *The Rocker Miner,* September 13, 1930, p. 2.

53. *Ibid.*

54. *Rock Springs Miner,* July 11, 1930, p. 1. See also October 3, 1930 issue for a discussion of Rock Springs being put on the eastbound air mail schedule.

55. *Rock Springs Miner,* February 12, 1931, p. 1.

56. CRM, No. 29, 63-64.

57. *Ibid.,* 64.

58. *Ibid.*

59. CRM No. 19.

60. *Ibid.*

61. CRM, No. 29, 39.

62. *Ibid.,* 40.

63. *Ibid.,* 41.

64. Gardner and Flores, *Forgotten Frontier.*

65. CRM, No. 29, 39.

66. *Ibid.*

67. "Green River, A Community that Serves the World's Need for Soda Ash," Ms. on file, Sweetwater County Museum, Green River, 4; *Wyoming Mineral and Energy Year Book* (Cheyenne: Department of Commerce, 1991), 42-43.

68. *Ibid.*

69. *Wyoming Mineral and Energy Year Book,* 42-43.

70. *Ibid.*

71. *Ibid.,* 97.

72. *Ibid.*

73. *Ibid.*

74. Kathy Gilbert, "History of Mountain Fuels," Manuscripts on 20th Century U.S. West, Western Wyoming College, Spring 1992, Ms on file Archaeological Services, Western Wyoming College.

75. *Casper Star Tribune,* December 1, 1992, p. 1.

76. In 1873, there were 1,000 Eastern Shoshone, in "Population," *Great Basin* (Washington: Smithsonian Institution, 1986), 608. In 1824, before removal, the Cherokee population was 14,972. [New Echota, Georgia] *Cherokee Phoenix,* June 18, 1828.

77. Gretel Ehrlich, *The Solace of Open Spaces* (New York: Penguin Press, 1985)

Conclusion

1. T. N. Wallace Stegner, *The American West* as Living Space (Ann Arbor: The University of Michigan Press, 1987), 23-24.

2. *Ibid.,* 24.

3. *Ibid.,* 25.

Index

A. Dudley Gardner is a historical archaeologist and associate professor of history at Western Wyoming Community College. He is a member of the Wyoming Governor's Consulting Committee on National Register of Historic Places. Among his publications are: a work co-authored with Verla R. Flores, *Forgotten Frontier, A History of Wyoming Coal Mining*; a work co-authored with Val Brinkerhoff, *An American Place: A Centennial Portrait of Rock Springs, Wyomimg, Then and Now, 1889–1989*; and he was the senior author of *The Bear River Divide,* a portion of the historic Oregon Trail. He resides in Rock Springs with Jodie and their two children.

Val Brinkerhoff has taught photography for Western Wyoming Community College since 1980. He holds a degree in art and in photography. He has done extensive research and creative work in hand coloring, toning, and other experimental image-making techniques in which he teaches workshops throughout the Intermountain region. He has previously published *An American Place: A Centennial Portrait of Rock Springs, Wyoming, Then and Now, 1889–1989* with A. Dudley Gardner. Val has exhibited and published his works widely. He resides in Rock Springs with Trina and their four children.